Interpreting the Legacy of Women's Suffrage at Museums and Historic Sites

AASLH

INTERPRETING HISTORY

ABOUT THE ORGANIZATION

The American Association for State and Local History (AASLH) is a national history membership association headquartered in Nashville, Tennessee, that provides leadership and support for its members who preserve and interpret state and local history in order to make the past more meaningful to all people. AASLH members are leaders in preserving, researching, and interpreting traces of the American past to connect the people, thoughts, and events of yesterday with the creative memories and abiding concerns of people, communities, and our nation today. In addition to sponsorship of this book series, AASLH publishes *History News* magazine, a newsletter, technical leaflets and reports, and other materials; confers prizes and awards in recognition of outstanding achievement in the field; supports a broad education program and other activities designed to help members work more effectively; and advocates on behalf of the discipline of history. To join AASLH, go to www.aaslh.org or contact Membership Services, AASLH, 2021 21st Ave. South, Suite 320, Nashville, TN 37212.

ABOUT THE SERIES

The American Association for State and Local History publishes the *Interpreting History* series in order to provide expert, in-depth guidance in interpretation for history professionals at museums and historic sites. The books are intended to help practitioners expand their interpretation to be more inclusive of the range of American history.

Books in this series help readers:

- quickly learn about the questions surrounding a specific topic,
- introduce them to the challenges of interpreting this part of history, and
- highlight best practice examples of how interpretation has been done by different organizations.

They enable institutions to place their interpretative efforts into a larger context, despite each having a specific and often localized mission. These books serve as quick references to practical considerations, further research, and historical information.

TITLES IN THE SERIES

1. *Interpreting Native American History and Culture at Museums and Historic Sites* by Raney Bench
2. *Interpreting the Prohibition Era at Museums and Historic Sites* by Jason D. Lantzer
3. *Interpreting African American History and Culture at Museums and Historic Sites* by Max van Balgooy
4. *Interpreting LGBT History at Museums and Historic Sites* by Susan Ferentinos
5. *Interpreting Slavery at Museums and Historic Sites* by Kristin L. Gallas and James De-Wolf Perry
6. *Interpreting Food at Museums and Historic Sites* by Michelle Moon
7. *Interpreting Difficult History at Museums and Historic Sites* by Julia Rose
8. *Interpreting American Military History at Museums and Historic Sites* by Marc K. Blackburn
9. *Interpreting Naval History at Museums and Historic Sites* by Benjamin J. Hruska
10. *Interpreting Anniversaries and Milestones at Museums and Historic Sites* by Kimberly A. Kenney
11. *Interpreting American Jewish History at Museums and Historic Sites* by Avi Y. Decter
12. *Interpreting Agriculture at Museums and Historic Sites* by Debra A. Reid
13. *Interpreting Maritime History at Museums and Historic Sites* by Joel Stone
14. *Interpreting the Civil War at Museums and Historic Sites* edited by Kevin M. Levin
15. *Interpreting Immigration at Museums and Historic Sites* edited by Dina A. Bailey
16. *Interpreting the Legacy of Women's Suffrage at Museums and Historic Sites* by Page Harrington

Interpreting the Legacy of Women's Suffrage at Museums and Historic Sites

Page Harrington

ROWMAN & LITTLEFIELD
Lanham • Boulder • New York • London

Published by Rowman & Littlefield
An imprint of The Rowman & Littlefield Publishing Group, Inc.
4501 Forbes Boulevard, Suite 200, Lanham, Maryland 20706
www.rowman.com

86–90 Paul Street, London EC2A 4NE, United Kingdom

British Library Cataloguing in Publication Information Available

Library of Congress Cataloging-in-Publication Data Available

ISBN 978-1-5381-1876-4 (cloth. : alk. paper)
ISBN 978-1-5381-1877-1 (pbk. : alk. paper)
ISBN 978-1-5381-1878-8 (electronic)

∞™ The paper used in this publication meets the minimum requirements of American National Standard for Information Sciences—Permanence of Paper for Printed Library Materials, ANSI/NISO Z39.48-1992.

For Jeff, Haley, and Jeff T.

aka "Clan Harrington"

Contents

Acknowledgments

Within my first few months as the executive director of the Sewall-Belmont House and Museum, Jennifer Krafchik, who was the collection manager, and I began to discuss updating the exhibits and tour script. Even though expanding the public content to include the work of African American suffragists was a high priority, we were unsure where and how to begin and so the effort stalled. This book explores the reasons behind that failed attempt, but it also highlights many other projects that were successful due to the collaborative efforts of those individuals and organizations. If there is one overarching "lesson learned," it is that without a professional and personal support network to rely on, many large projects—including this book—would not be possible.

I am fortunate to have a strong network of both friends and colleagues. To begin, I am grateful to Jennifer Krafchik for sharing her deep knowledge of suffrage history, for her constant support, and for being a great friend. My understanding of how racism impacted the women's suffrage movement was greatly influenced by Dr. Rosalyn Terborg-Penn. I was fortunate to have the opportunity to work with her on two public programs during my tenure at Sewall-Belmont House, and perhaps more than anyone she truly changed the way I thought about racism within the suffrage movement and beyond. Her death in 2018 created a significant void not only in our work around the centennial of 2020 but also within the women's history field going forward.

I have been fortunate to know Kyle E. Ciani and Cindi Malinick for more than twenty years. I can always rely on them for support, advice, and friendship. Kyle provided a lifeline more than once, as she never failed to quickly respond to a 911 text about book content, or to gently remind me that I am "only human" and so should give myself a break from time to time. I am also grateful to Allida Black, who challenged my understanding of the women of the NWP and became a true friend along the way.

My thanks to Noelle Trent, Krysta Jones, Janedra Sykes, and Cindy Grisham, who allowed me to pepper them with questions about their work, and then share examples of their expertise throughout the book. I am also grateful to Chitra Panjabi for allowing me to tell her story from the 2016 national monument designation. I am indebted to my colleagues who shared challenges and successes through their case studies—Jennifer Krafchik, Alyssa Constad, Lori Osborne, and Rebecca Price. The case studies highlight their dedication to revealing the history of racism at their institutions and also serve as strong examples for others who wish to undertake this work. This manuscript is better because of their work and I remain grateful for their efforts. I am also fortunate to sit on several history committees, including the scholar committee of the National Votes for Women's Trail led by Judith Wellman, the steering committee of the Women's Vote Centennial Initiative, and the Women's History Affinity Community of AASLH. My fellow committee members are brilliant and tenacious, and it is a pleasure to serve alongside them and also learn from them.

My heartfelt thanks to Sue Ferentinos, who was the first to suggest that I expand this content into a book, and Bob Beatty's early encouragement gave me the confidence to take on a project of this magnitude. John Dichtl and Aja Bain from AASLH were always supportive and helpful, and I truly appreciate the comments and suggestions offered through the peer review process. I am grateful to Sarah Pharaon, who offered encouragement and advice, and volunteered (!) to produce the International Coalition of Sites of Conscience Voting Rights Discussion Guide for use in the book. My thanks also to Charles Harmon and Erinn Slanina from Rowman & Littlefield, as well as Rebecca Shrum and Taylor Kiland, who helped guide and offered sage advice on the world of publishing. I am also indebted to Kelsey Millay, Hannah Craddock, and Alana Dunn, for their diligent research, resource checking, and sharp editing skills. I owe a debt of gratitude to Margaret Puskar-Pasewicz for her interest in this book, her sharp developmental editing skills, and positive comments throughout the editing process, which meant so much to me.

Many others contributed to my overall understanding of the suffrage and women's rights movements and took the time to answer questions and share valuable resources. This includes Nancy Tate, Felicia Bell, Kathleen Pate, Sarah Jenks, Joy Kinard, Cathleen Cahill, Ann Lewis, Sarah Seidman, Mary van Balgooy, Marjorie Spruill, Robyn Muncy, Lisa Kathleen Graddy, Elizabeth Maurer, Janice Ruth, Kathryn White, Sherryl Lang, Liz Harper, Corinne Porter, Estevan Rael-Gálvez, Lucy Beard, A'Lelia Bundles, Virginia Kase, Fredie Kay, Krissah Thompson, Susan Philpott, Jana Friesen-McCabe, Essence McDowell, Pat Mooney Melvin, Barbara Howe, Judy Wellman, Jessica Tava, Earnestine Jenkins, Coline Jenkins, Molly Murphy MacGregor, Jill Zahniser, and Robert Cooney.

And finally, this would not have been possible without the constant encouragement and support of my family—Claudia Gerkin, Cleone Gerkin, HeiDee DeStefano, Noah and Sarah Springfield, Haley Harrington-Thomas, and Jeff Thomas. Finally, my husband Jeff—neither of us could have imagined that my decision to write this book would essentially amount to having a "second job" that consumed most nights and weekends. I am truly grateful for his constant support, love, encouragement, as well as doing the majority of the cooking, shopping, and cleaning, which made it possible for me to tackle such a daunting project.

List of Illustrations

CHAPTER 1

A New Executive Director's Dilemma

I N 2008 I BEGAN MY NINE-YEAR TENURE as the executive director of the Sewall-Belmont House and Museum (SBHM) in Washington, DC. Working for one of the premier women's history sites in the country that focused exclusively on suffrage and women's equality was an exciting prospect, one made even more memorable as my tenure began on Women's Equality Day. The Nineteenth Amendment to the U.S. Constitution had been signed into law exactly eighty-eight years earlier.[1] The museum, which began operating as the Sewall-Belmont House and Museum in the late 1990s, interpreted the history of the National Woman's Party (NWP).[2] Founded in the final years before the passage of the Nineteenth Amendment, the NWP brought controversial tactics such as picketing the White House to their work for women's enfranchisement. Over the next five decades, NWP members wrote and lobbied for hundreds of legislative measures, including the Equal Rights Amendment (ERA).[3]

When I began at SBHM, the institution was struggling financially and had a staff of only three full-time employees and a handful of part-time docents. The stock market downturn resulting in the global financial crisis had significant ramifications for SBHM as well as many other institutions. Given the increased financial insecurity, I made it a priority to introduce myself to donors and stakeholders in an effort to begin building key relationships.

One of my first meetings was with Dr. Allida Black, a noted scholar of Eleanor Roosevelt, ardent feminist, and longtime museum stakeholder. Barely five minutes into our conversation, she interjected, "She was a racist, you know? Alice."[4] I assumed correctly that Dr. Black was referring to the resistance to African American women's participation in the Woman's Suffrage Procession of 1913. Organized by the NWP and held on the eve of President-elect Woodrow Wilson's inauguration in Washington, DC, African American suffragists were expected to march at the back of the procession to appease the southern Whites.

As a newly hired executive director, I was nowhere near ready to broach this topic during our introductory meeting. Nor could I imagine the extent to which her assertion about the racism of Alice Paul and other NWP leaders would influence my long-term work at SBHM. Initially caught off guard, and unsure how to respond, I replied that it was my

Figure 1.1. Belmont-Paul Women's Equality National Monument, formerly the Sewall-Belmont House. Photo courtesy of The National Woman's Party

intention to fully explore the controversial history of the NWP and also ensure that the SBHM moved toward a sustainable financial future. In hindsight, however, the two goals were never given equal weight; the constant financial struggles and physical deterioration of the building provided frequent excuses for me to avoid pursuing the more controversial side of NWP history. Looking back, I realize that my inaction allowed an already narrowly focused historical interpretation of women's suffrage to continue unchecked for almost another decade.

The meeting ended amicably, and during my tenure Dr. Black became a trusted advisor, friend, and stalwart museum supporter. This initial conversation—and my uncertainty about how to begin broadening the historic narrative to include the racism within the suffrage movement—served as the impetus for many thought-provoking discussions with friends and colleagues from other women's history sites. These conversations allowed us to begin a tacit exploration of the complicated racial tensions that exist within U.S. women's history. While we never second-guessed the need to explore this critical issue at our respective institutions, we were all unsure how to begin a public dialogue. Furthermore, we feared that we had insufficient knowledge to navigate the sensitive topic.

In the last thirteen years, my understanding of the history of the NWP as well as Alice Paul's leadership and vision has evolved. I remain unwavering in my belief that the women of the NWP were courageous, tenacious, and brilliant political strategists. They also played a critical role in expanding women's rights with the introduction of the ERA. However, the NWP's narrow mission and continued marginalization of the Black women who worked alongside them nonetheless set the stage for a historical narrative that still largely excludes the accomplishments of many women of color. That said, the NWP's use of racist discourse and practices in their work for enfranchisement does not wholly invalidate the overarching value of that work. Instead, both are true and viewed together give us greater insight into the complexity, value, and limitations of the U.S. women's suffrage movement.

While it may be disheartening and even painful for some to acknowledge that racism was prevalent in the suffrage movement, denying its existence serves no credible purpose. As practitioners, we must move forward to increase our own knowledge so that we are able to better interpret this nuanced history with our visitors. The case studies contained in this book provide useful examples from our colleagues who have faced these challenges.

What to Expect from This Book

As with the other books in the Interpreting History series from Rowman & Littlefield and the American Association of State and Local History (AASLH), this book is geared toward those who interpret history for the public at museums and historic sites. The overarching goal is to encourage and support practitioners to think more expansively about suffrage history by including all aspects of women's enfranchisement—concerns and disputes around citizenship, democracy, voting rights, civil rights, and social justice. This new perspective will hopefully lead to productive conversations at their museums and historic sites.

To begin, we will take a look at past suffrage celebrations in 1945, 1970, 1995, and 2020 and the key cultural and political events that influenced them. Additionally, a series of case studies "takes the pulse" of the General Federation of Women's Clubs (GFWC), the National Woman's Party (NWP), and the Frances Willard House Museum (FWHM), all women's organizations that have existed for more than a century, as they explored race and racism within their own institutional history. The final case study on the "March to the Nineteenth" program by Chick History provides a valuable example of how a non-site-based history organization can contribute to and advance the ongoing work in this field.

The number of new books, articles, museum exhibitions, and conference sessions reexamining the significance as well as legislative inadequacies of the Nineteenth Amendment have increased in the last few years. This is unsurprising given the excitement around the centennial and the need for a deeper look into the campaigns for suffrage. With these resources readily available, *Interpreting the Legacy of Women's Suffrage at Museums and History Sites* will share practical tips and advice for incorporating this new material into educational programs at museums of all sizes. Additional materials include a Front Page Dialogue guide by the International Coalition of Sites of Conscience on facilitating group discussions around voting rights and the AASLH Nineteenth Amendment Value Statement, which offers in-depth guidance for interpretation.

One of the most frustrating challenges that I faced during my tenure at SBHM was the difficulty in locating materials, both primary and secondary sources that document the history of women of color and their work for enfranchisement. Because others in the field have encountered similar challenges, I include a comprehensive timeline that begins with the U.S. Constitution in 1787. This timeline identifies milestones in voting rights, abolition, immigration, and labor unions as well as women's clubs and Black sororities. It also notes the founding of influential organizations such as the National Association of Colored Women, Women's Trade Union League, and National Council of Jewish Women. Also provided is a compilation of online materials that includes women of color and their work for social justice. Many of these resources were new to me, and I share them with the hope that they prompt new discussions in our field that result in more inclusive, diverse, and historically accurate narratives of the suffrage movement and U.S. women's political activism moving forward.

Clarifying Terminology

By the late 1890s, gender stereotypes were being discussed and dismantled. More than ever before, women were attending college, achieving some financial independence, and attempting to change their world by promoting suffrage, temperance, and other progressive reforms. Historically referred to in the singular as *woman's suffrage*, the meaning relates directly to the idea of the "new woman" who self-identified as a progressive, civic-minded participant in her community. This term prompted women to self-identify as an educated and engaged individual, rather than just a passive participant. When referring to historic events or ideas, I will use the term *woman's suffrage*; however, because the term now sounds dated, when discussing contemporary themes or events, I will use the more modern term, *women's suffrage*.

Another term that is frequently misused is *suffragette*. The American women who traveled to England to work for suffrage, then continued their work at home, largely self-identified as suffragists, while their British contemporaries self-identified as suffragettes. The British term began as a derogatory label bestowed on women in the press. The women then adopted the term as a way to take control of their image and narrate their own story. While to some the terms are interchangeable, I prefer to remain consistent with the majority of American women who self-identified as suffragists.

Kimberlé Crenshaw coined the term *intersectionality*, the practice of examining the interface between race and gender in feminist theory, more than three decades ago. A professor of law at Columbia Law School and the University of California, Los Angeles, Crenshaw wanted to "define this profound invisibility in relation to the law. Racial and gender discrimination overlapped not only in the workplace but in other arenas of life; equally significant, these burdens were almost completely absent from feminist and anti-racist advocacy which contributed to the racial divide within the women's advocacy movements of today."[5] Public historians and practitioners use this framework to examine how race, gender, class, and other social positions can both enable a person's actions while simultaneously creating other barriers. In practical terms, using an intersectional approach in our work means that we recognize that every individual faces a unique set of social factors that shape their lives. Not recognizing that these factors exist leads to an incomplete understanding and therefore inaccurate interpretations in our exhibits and programs.[6]

The initial concept for this book originated from my professional experience at SBHM, which had a singular focus on the national suffrage campaign of the early twentieth century and largely avoided discussing the racial tensions that existed between White and Black women in the northeastern United States. I recognize now that this narrow focus was even more limited than I originally thought. Using a binary narrative of Black and White women implies that it is the only history tainted by racism. We know that this is simply untrue. The work for women's enfranchisement played out across the country and was impacted by regional views on race and ethnicity. Widespread xenophobia and ethnocentrism affected immigration laws and restricted citizenship, which also influenced the lives of Hispanic, Chinese, and Indigenous women and men.

Given all of the advanced scholarship and resources available to us, it is without question that racism was omnipresent in late-nineteenth-century American society—whether it was acknowledged as such, or couched under the tired trope "she was a product of her time." Going forward, it is my hope that when practitioners and educators are given a chance to recognize the underlying racism in our historical narratives, they call it out for what it was: systemic racism within the women's suffrage movement.

Notes

1. The Nineteenth Amendment was signed in to law on August 26, 1920. In 1973 the U.S. Congress designated the day as Women's Equality Day, typically marked by a presidential proclamation. Communities celebrate the day through local and national events and programs. "Women's Equality Day," National Women's History Alliance, accessed September 2, 2020, https://nationalwomenshistoryalliance.org/resources/commemorations/womens-equality -day.
2. The SBHM operated independently until April 12, 2016, when it was designated as the Belmont-Paul Women's Equality National Monument and the National Park Service assumed ownership and responsibility for day-to-day operations. For text of the full proclamation, see Barack Obama, "Presidential Proclamation—Establishment of the Belmont-Paul Women's Equality National Monument," News Release, April 12, 2016, https://obamawhitehouse .archives.gov/the-press-office/2016/04/12/presidential-proclamation-establishment-belmont -paul-womens-equality.
3. The house located at the corner of 2nd and Constitution NE became the fifth and final headquarters of the National Woman's Party, which grew out of the Congressional Union of the National American Woman Suffrage Association (NAWSA) and was founded by Alice Paul in 1916.
4. In subsequent conversations with Dr. Black, she has expanded on her initial thoughts, clarifying that "I don't use that word often" in regards to her unapologetic use of the word *racist*. Allida Black, interview with author, January 15, 2019.
5. Kimberlé Crenshaw, "Why Intersectionality Can't Wait," *Washington Post*, September 24, 2015, www.washingtonpost.com/news/in-theory/wp/2015/09/24/why-intersectional ity-cant-wait.
6. For more information, see Jennifer C. Nash, *Black Feminism Reimagined: After Intersectionality* (Durham, NC: Duke University Press, 2019); Paula Birnbaum, "Practicing What We Preach," American Alliance of Museums, March 1, 2020, www.aam-us.org/2020/03/01/ practicing-what-we-preach; and Peter Kaufman, "Intersectionality for Beginners," *Everyday Sociology* (blog; W.W. Norton), April 23, 2018, www.everydaysociologyblog.com/2018/04/ intersectionality-for-beginners.html.

CHAPTER 2

Expanding and Reframing Women's Suffrage

THE CENTENNIAL COMMEMORATION of the ratification of the Nineteenth Amendment in 2020 provided a nascent opportunity for some museums and historic sites to share a more inclusive narrative of women's enfranchisement in America. This expanded narrative brought to the forefront the many examples of inequality and racism throughout the long history of the campaigns for women's suffrage. This also allowed us to deviate from the traditional storyline that begins with the Women's Rights Convention in Seneca Falls held in July of 1848. The event featured speakers Elizabeth Cady Stanton, Lucretia Mott, and Frederick Douglass, among many others, and is often erroneously referred to as the definitive beginning of suffrage. This storyline chronicles the major suffrage organizations and their support or opposition to the Fifteenth Amendment, the suffragists who picketed the White House and were subsequently imprisoned, and ends with the final push in Nashville resulting in the ratification of the Nineteenth Amendment in 1920.[1]

This narrative, which condenses the movement from 1848 to 1920, is ingrained at least in part due to the work of Elizabeth Cady Stanton, Susan B. Anthony, Matilda Jocelyn Gage, and Ida Husted Harper, who began work on the six-volume *History of Woman Suffrage* in 1881. Finally completed in 1922, more than twenty years after Stanton's death, it became a widely cited compendium on the early women's movement. It also ensured that both Stanton and Anthony would be recognized as leaders of the suffrage movement long into the future, and conversely pushed others into the shadows.

Sally Roesch Wagner, a historian of women's suffrage, reminds us "movements don't have a beginning and an end" and thus encourages us to move beyond the well-known 1848 to 1920 timeline.[2] Wagner reaffirms that women's enfranchisement was a long and circuitous path that began before the founding of our nation and before voting rights for women were purposely left out of the U.S. Constitution. Expanding our timeline to pre-1848 is critical; however, it is also imperative to include a discussion on voting rights and enfranchisement post 1920. While the Nineteenth Amendment removed the gender restriction to voting at the national level, a number of women—including some women of color—were already able to cast their vote in more than twenty states.[3]

In spite of the new amendment, Jim Crow laws expanded and further restricted Black women's as well as men's voting access after 1920. For many African Americans, the battle for enfranchisement continued until the Voting Rights Act of 1965. Going forward, it is important that we adopt an expanded chronology, in essence reframing the narrative of women's enfranchisement. This will allow us to view the women's suffrage movement in its totality, confirming that it was a series of highly charged and polarizing political campaigns complicated by race, class, and regional differences as well as the ambitions and agendas of the various leadership factions.[4]

In the years since 1970, historians have worked to broaden the interpretation of suffrage through their research and publications.[5] This scholarship has allowed practitioners and public historians to share this updated history at museums and historic sites of all sizes. Examples of exhibits featuring a more inclusive and expanded narrative were showcased at prominent institutions such as the Library of Congress, the National Portrait Gallery, and the National Archives in Washington, DC.[6] These exhibits and the accompanying public programs highlighted the experiences of the many women of color whose contributions have largely been omitted from the celebrations of past anniversaries. We must now foster this expanded narrative and ensure that it is widely disseminated through the programmatic offerings at museums and historic sites of all sizes.

While exhibitions featuring an expanded narrative have thus far been spearheaded by a handful of prominent museums and scholars, there are also examples from small museums with more limited resources. During Women's History Month in 2019, former president of the Arkansas Women's History Initiative (AWHI) Kathleen Pate brought to fruition a creative four-way partnership between the AWHI, the MacArthur Museum of Arkansas Military History (MMAMH), the Arkansas Museums Association (AMA), and the Butler Center for Arkansas Studies of the Central Arkansas Library System (CALS). In speaking to the overarching value of the alliance, Pate says, "Partnering with other cultural institutions allowed us to reach a variety of new audiences. The collaboration grew out of necessity because no one organization had the resources to pull off the entire project. By working together we connected with Arkansans across the state and shared valuable content."[7]

The partnership produced three local events and one exhibition that ran simultaneously. The exhibit "Imagery and Irony: The Battle for Women's Suffrage Through the Political Cartoons of Nina Allender" at the MMAMH, located in downtown Little Rock, featured framed reproductions of Allender's cartoons and drew parallels between the political cartoons of suffragist Nina Allender and the World War I propaganda posters from their permanent collection.[8] Many of the museum visitors were previously unaware that Allender relied heavily on the iconic imagery of WWI, which allowed her to use the government's words against them in pointing out that while soldiers were fighting for democracy abroad, American women were still unable to cast their vote. The exhibit provided an atypical opportunity for MMAMH to introduce the history of women's enfranchisement to their visitors.

As part of the opening reception, MMAMH also hosted a lecture "Interpreting the Legacy of Suffrage," which in addition to providing an in-depth analysis of the importance

Figure 2.1. MacArthur Museum of Arkansas Military History "Imagery and Irony: The Battle for Women's Suffrage Through the Political Cartoons of Nina Allender" exhibit, taken March 28, 2019. Photo by author

Figure 2.2.   MacArthur Museum of Arkansas Military History "Imagery and Irony: The Battle for Women's Suffrage Through the Political Cartoons of Nina Allender" exhibit, taken March 28, 2019. Photo by author

of Allender's work, introduced the audience to the need for expanding the traditional narrative around women's suffrage. The Betsey Wright Distinguished Lecture at CALS expanded the content even further with a presentation and lively Q&A titled "Suffrage & Race Relations: A Divided Legacy." In the keynote for the AMA, where the audience was comprised of museum practitioners from across the state, the content included examples of tactics used to effectively garner support from organization stakeholders and leadership, specifically for those who faced opposition as they worked to introduce new women's history content to their audiences.[9] Taken together, the series of events brought new content to the audiences of each of the four partners, made possible only through sharing the program expenses. The content examined the racism of the suffragists, discussed the need for expanding beyond the 1848–1920 narrative, and challenged the misconception that women's history falls outside the accepted content parameters of a military museum.

To recognize the centennial, small to mid-size museums also took advantage of traveling exhibits that enable the sharing of content without the expense of curating and installing a physical exhibit. There were multiple organizations that produced content, among them the Standing Committee on the Law Library of Congress, which offers educational programming for the American Bar Association. They curated and made available a six-panel exhibition titled "100 Years after the 19th Amendment: Their Legacy, and Our Future," which traveled to more than 150 locations between 2019 and 2021. Additionally, the National Archives, in partnership with the Women's Suffrage Centennial Commission, the National Archives Foundation, and their sponsors, provided free of charge more than 4,500 "Rightfully Hers" pop-up displays to museums, schools, and other organizations. While size constraints did reduce the quantity of content, the low price point and easy installation served to introduce the public across the country to the narrative of women's suffrage and enfranchisement.[10]

Obstacles to Building an Inclusive Narrative

While reinterpreting the history of women's suffrage and promoting this new work are important goals, there are often significant barriers. First, a museum practitioner's heavy day-to-day workload can make it a challenge to find time to begin a new project. There are also repercussions such as facing criticism from peers, donors, and the public, which can be an even more formidable challenge. Even so it is also not an insurmountable obstacle to our goal of fostering a new national narrative of women's enfranchisement.

The path to dismantling criticism begins by understanding the motivation behind it. There are those who question the reason for expanding the traditional narrative to include the geographic and economic differences, as well as the racism of the campaigns. They believe that openly exploring the prejudices of White suffragists and asserting that their words or actions fell short of our contemporary expectations somehow lessen their tremendous personal sacrifice and historic accomplishments. Understanding this point of view allows us to provide clarity around the reason for sharing a new narrative. Ultimately, it is not about portraying any individual as singularly "good" or "bad" or highlighting negative actions.[11] Instead, by expanding the narrative, we offer a more complete understanding of the arc of the history and provide context to the words and actions of the suffragists. In doing so, we correct a sentimental and inaccurate narrative that has erased racism and discrimination within the history of the movement and reveal the accomplishments of women of color.[12] With an entire century to reflect back on, the time has come to give the venerated stories we once believed to be inscrutable a fresh look through a twenty-first-century lens.

Envisioning Change at Museums, Historic Sites, and Beyond

As we look ahead, there are multiple opportunities to expand and reframe the scope of our work from centering solely on suffrage to including the historic campaigns on the expansion of political rights of all women, including Black, Indigenous, and people of color (BIPOC), and members of the LGBTQ community, as well as debates over citizenship and immigration reform. First the centennial of the introduction of the ERA will occur in 2023. The following year, we mark the centennial of the Indian Citizenship Act, which granted U.S. citizenship to Indigenous people. Furthermore, in 2026, we will mark the 250th anniversary of American independence.[13] Each of these anniversaries presents an opportunity for museums and historic sites to promote an in-depth dialogue around women's enfranchisement, citizenship, voting rights, and social justice efforts. As public historians and practitioners, we have the ability to share a more nuanced understanding of how democracy works in America, which includes who is allowed to take part in the democratic process and who is not.

In addition to sharing this content at historic sites and museums, we should expand our focus to include the local libraries, schools, League of Women Voters chapters, Girl Scout troops, and professional organizations that incorporated the history of women's suffrage into their programs and events in 2020. Going forward these organizations can also benefit from our work, and even share it with their members and supporters. Some organizations may also be able to begin confronting systemic racism and expanding their understanding of women's political activity; however, this requires an unwavering staff commitment and buy-in from leadership and stakeholders. The case studies in chapters 5, 6, and 7 provide in-depth examples and offer valuable insight into their process.

The League of Women Voters of the United States (LWVUS) provides a recent example of how a national organization has successfully confronted their past, which includes racism.[14] In a 2018 blog post penned within the first few months of her tenure, Virginia Kase, the CEO of LWVUS, responded to a widely read *New York Times* op-ed by Brent Staples.[15] Her post, titled "Facing Hard Truths about the League's Origin," calls out the racist actions and rhetoric of White suffragists, including LWVUS founder Carrie Chapman Catt.[16] In speaking about past actions of the league, Kase quotes Catt's highly controversial discriminatory statement: "White supremacy will be strengthened, not weakened, by women's suffrage." Instead of making excuses, Kase states without apology that Catt was "a complicated character, a political operative, and by modern standards, yes, racist."[17] Addressing one of the most controversial aspects of the group's history, Kase writes, "Today, we acknowledge this shortcoming and that we have more work to do" and notes the LWVUS's new diversity, equity, and inclusion policy. She concludes with a public pledge: "As we continue to grow our movement, we acknowledge our privilege and must use our power to raise the voices of those who haven't always had a seat at the table."[18]

The message put forth by the LWVUS was both bold and prescient. Recognizing the need for change, and moving forward to implement that change on an organization-wide scale, is laudable, and hopefully others will be inspired to follow Kase's lead. That said, not all museums and historic sites will choose to be as bold as the LWVUS; many institutions will take a more nuanced, and even multi-phased, approach toward implementing a change in narrative and focus. Whether the work moves quickly or unfolds slowly over time, organizations and historic sites grappling with women's political history need to initiate discussions about systemic racism and determine how to expand their narratives within the parameters of their mission, vision, and community expectations. These topics are explored in more detail in upcoming chapters and case studies.

Resources for the Public History Field

Once the decision has been made to expand and reframe the narrative, it is time to begin exploring content. Finding the historical content needed to reimagine this narrative can be time consuming, but there are valuable resources widely accessible to practitioners. For example, AASLH has produced the Centennial of the Nineteenth Amendment Value Statement produced by the Women's History Affinity Community (WHAC).[19] The statement originated from the recognition that the public history field needed guidance on how to incorporate difficult topics, such as racial, economic, religious, and political tensions, within their program content. In an effort to further understand the needs of fellow practitioners, during the summer of 2018 WHAC offered public historians and practitioners time to complete an online survey asking about their work and efforts around the centennial.[20]

The survey yielded over one hundred responses and served as the baseline for the "Telling the Truth about Suffrage" roundtable and small-group working session during the 2018 AASLH Annual Meeting, which ultimately helped to shape its AASLH Nineteenth Amendment Centennial Value Statement. More than two-thirds of respondents indicated they would focus on diversity and inclusion efforts and, if possible, would include content from the Civil Rights era to post-2016 presidential election and beyond. The survey also illuminated challenges that were common among the participating sites, including the difficulty in identifying diverse content due to limited archival holdings for women's suffrage and, in particular, those highlighting women of color.

Released in May 2019, the value statement includes seven guiding principles that serve both as a key part of the statement and as a framework of terms and ideas to be used as discussion topics.[21] Overall, the statement "presents an opportunity to expand the narrative

Figure 2.3.   Telling the Truth about Suffrage roundtable at the AASLH annual meeting in 2018. Photo courtesy of Kelsey Millay

of women's suffrage; challenge preconceptions and definitions about history; and engage with the proud, conflicted, and complex realities of our shared history." In addition to the guiding principles, the statement also includes more than twenty questions that, when used as starting points, will allow practitioners to "apply diverse, inclusive, and intersectional approaches" to their work.[22]

Another resource is the timeline offered in this book, which provides a compilation of key efforts around voting rights and citizenship issues. This timeline chronicles the contributions by organizations advocating for abolition, temperance, Indigenous rights, women's equality, and the labor movement as well as the events related to the expansion of education and sororities, LGBTQ equality efforts, civil rights, and women in politics. This timeline has a dual benefit: first, it offers practical starting points to consider as public historians explore new content and make connections to their local history; and second, it enables discussions around the totality of the suffrage movement, including the ramifications of the sheer unevenness of how voting rights have been granted throughout our history.

Going forward, public historians and museum practitioners are in a position to offer careful analysis and act as thought leaders to guide the challenging dialogue around racism and inequality. An essential piece of this work is ensuring that museums and historic sites refrain from using the limited narrative of 1848 to 1920, which showcases mostly White women celebrating their right to vote without acknowledging the deeply divisive and racially oppressive tactics used in part to secure that right. Organizations outside of the history field such as the LWVUS and local schools and libraries also have the potential to be part of the dialogue. Working with our colleagues across sectors and disciplines, we can enhance the public understanding of the work for women's enfranchisement, political equality, voting rights, democracy, and citizenship and ensure that a more inclusive narrative is shared widely going forward.

Notes

1. The amendment passed by both the U.S. House of Representatives and U.S. Senate in 1919. On August 18, 1920, Tennessee became the thirty-sixth state to ratify, and it was signed into law on August 26, 1920, by Secretary of State Bainbridge Colby. For more information, see "State-by-State Race to Ratification of the 19th Amendment," Women's History, National Park Service, www.nps.gov/subjects/womenshistory/womens-suffrage-timeline.htm.
2. Sally Roesch Wagner, ed., *The Women's Suffrage Movement* (London: Penguin, 2019), xxii.
3. For additional publications on women's suffrage and voting rights, see also Marjorie J. Spruill, *Divided We Stand: The Battle for Women's Rights and Family Values That Polarized American Politics* (New York: Bloomsbury, 2017); Susan Ware, *Why They Marched: Untold Stories of the Women Who Fought for the Right to Vote* (Cambridge, MA: Harvard University Press, 2019); Lisa Tetrault, *The Myth of Seneca Falls: Memory and the Women's Suffrage Movement, 1848–1898* (Chapel Hill: University of North Carolina Press, 2014); Martha Jones, *Vanguard: How Black Women Broke Barriers, Won the Vote, and Insisted on Equality for All* (New York: Basic Books, 2020); Ellen Carol DuBois, *Suffrage: Women's Long Battle for the Vote* (New York: Simon and Schuster, 2020); Cathleen Cahill, *Recasting the Vote: How Women of Color Transformed the Suffrage Movement* (Chapel Hill: University of North Carolina Press, 2020).

4. Wyoming territory constitution grants women the right to vote and to hold public office (1869); Colorado (1893); Utah and Idaho (1896); Washington State (1910); California (1911); Kansas, Oregon, and Arizona (1912); Alaska Territory (1913); Illinois—presidential elections only (1913); Montana and Nevada (1914); New York State (1917); Arkansas gives women the right to vote in primary, not general, elections (1917); Nebraska, North Dakota, Indiana, and Rhode Island grant women the right to partial suffrage (1917); South Dakota, Oklahoma, and Michigan (1918).

5. This version focuses primarily on the actions and work of the White women, which only tells a portion of the history. For more information, see Rosalyn Terborg-Penn, *African American Women in the Struggle for the Vote, 1850–1920* (Bloomington: Indiana University Press, 1998); Lori D. Ginzberg, *Elizabeth Cady Stanton: An American Life* (New York: Hill and Wang, 2009); Tetrault, *Myth of Seneca Falls*; Wagner, *Women's Suffrage Movement*; Jones, *Vanguard*; and Cahill, *Recasting the Vote*. Additional titles are included in bibliography.

6. For more information, see *Shall Not Be Denied: Women Fight for the Vote*, Library of Congress, accessed September 2, 2020, www.loc.gov/exhibitions/women-fight-for-the-vote/about-this-exhibition; "Votes for Women: A Portrait of Persistence," National Portrait Gallery, March 29, 2019–January 5, 2020, accessed September 2, 2020, https://npg.si.edu/exhibition/votes-for-women; and *Rightfully Hers: American Women and the Vote*, National Archives Museum, May 10, 2019–January 3, 2021, accessed September 2, 2020, https://museum.archives.gov/rightfully-hers.

7. Kathleen Pate, interview with the author, December 30, 2020.

8. Temporary Exhibits, City of Little Rock, accessed January 2021, www.littlerock.gov/for-residents/parks-and-recreation/macarthur-museum-of-arkansas-military-history/exhibits/temporary-exhibits.

9. Page Harrington, Keynote, Arkansas Museums Association, Little Rock, AR, March 2019.

10. For more information, see "*Rightfully Hers* Pop-Up Display," *Rightfully Hers: American Women and the Vote*, National Archives Museum, May 10, 2019–January 3, 2021, https://museum.archives.gov/rightfully-hers#popup; and "100 Years after the 19th Amendment: Their Legacy, and Our Future," Events, American Bar Association, accessed January 2021, www.americanbar.org/groups/public_interest/law_library_congress/events.

11. When speaking on this topic, I frequently get questions about the motive behind pointing out issues around race and racism within the suffrage movement. To some it seems counterproductive to highlight their faults instead of celebrating the accomplishments.

12. For more information, see Robin DiAngelo, *White Fragility: Why It's So Hard for White People to Talk about Racism* (Boston: Beacon Press, 2018), 2–4, 28–29, 71–73.

13. For more information, see Seth C. Bruggeman, ed., *Commemoration: The American Association for State and Local History Guide* (Lanham, MD: Rowman & Littlefield, 2017).

14. I am grateful to Virginia Kase, CEO of LWVUS, who took the time to speak with me and share her thoughts on the importance of their work.

15. Brent Staples, "How the Suffrage Movement Betrayed Black Women," *New York Times*, July 28, 2018, www.nytimes.com/2018/07/28/opinion/sunday/suffrage-movement-racism-black-women.html.

16. Virginia Kase and Chris Carson, "Facing Hard Truths about the League's Origins," *League of Women Voters* (blog), August 8, 2018, www.lwv.org/blog/facing-hard-truths-about-leagues-origin.

17. Kase and Carson, "Facing Hard Truths." Catt's quote is originally from Carrie Chapman Catt, "Objections to the Federal Amendment," in *Woman Suffrage by Federal Constitutional Amendment*, ed. Carrie Chapman Catt (New York: National Woman Suffrage, 1917), 76.

18. Kase and Carson, "Facing Hard Truths" (see note 8).

19. "AASLH 19th Amendment Centennial Value Statement," AASLH, accessed September 2, 2020, https://aaslh.org/19th-amendment-centennial-statement. Founded just after the 2014 Annual Meeting in St. Paul, Minnesota, WHAC began operating as a community group under the larger umbrella of AASLH. They envisioned a strong network for women's history practitioners to share both content and expertise as a valuable resource for practitioners in the field.

20. The survey launched in July 2018 through social media platforms, blog posts, and membership platforms.

21. The complete Value Statement is located in appendix C and on the AASLH website. "AASLH 19th Amendment Centennial Value Statement."

22. "AASLH 19th Amendment Centennial Value Statement."

CHAPTER 3

Milestones and Memorialization of Women's Suffrage

MAJOR ANNIVERSARIES PROVIDE A TIMELY opportunity for museums and historic sites to take a thoughtful and more inclusive look back at past events through a present-day lens. For many practitioners working in the public history field, these milestones offer a valuable opportunity to integrate new scholarship, address biases, and correct insensitive interpretations from the past. Nonetheless, as Seth Brugge-man—who writes about commemoration and planning historic anniversaries—reminds us, updating a well-recognized narrative can bring new challenges. While recent scholarship has deepened our understanding of the nuances of both the suffragists and their work, we may have also discovered that "our heroes were not so heroic or that our reasons for honoring them were not as pure as we'd like to believe."[1] Today we recognize that the overarching path to women's enfranchisement was circuitous, contentious, and awash with racial divisions. To understand the historic milestones that contributed to this contemporary viewpoint, we will briefly look back at the ways we celebrated the Nineteenth Amendment in 1945, 1970, and 1995.[2]

Barriers to Expanding Enfranchisement Post Civil War

At the conclusion of the Civil War in 1865, emancipation brought freedom to almost 4 million African Americans across the country. The Thirteenth, Fourteenth, and Fifteenth Amendments assured freedom, equal protection under the law, and voting rights for African American men. Enfranchisement brought African American men into the political realm as both voters and candidates for office. Wary of their growing influence, White political elites enacted poll taxes and literacy tests. Other efforts to keep them from the polls included escalating violence and lynching. As a result of these trends, voting registration numbers for

African Americans plummeted. Jim Crow practices—legally sanctioned racial segregation in public and private spaces—also expanded and thrived by the late nineteenth century.[3]

Founded in 1909, the National Association for the Advancement of Colored People devoted their efforts to lobbying and bringing legal suits to eliminate race-based discrimination across the country. Black clubwomen organized "citizenship schools" that offered information on citizens' rights, including strategies for avoiding legal and illegal barriers to voter registration as well as instruction for how to properly fill out a ballot.[4] While the Nineteenth Amendment, in theory, enfranchised women across the country in 1920, ongoing efforts to disenfranchise women of color quickly commenced. Although the amendment removed the gender restriction to voting, it did not guarantee any woman the right to vote. It would take almost fifty years of ongoing efforts to protect voting rights for women and men of color with the passage of the Voting Rights Act of 1965.

In addition to the continuing disenfranchisement of women of color, the powerful and unified block of women voters that suffrage leaders had long hoped for failed to materialize. Instead, in the first twenty years after the ratification of the Nineteenth Amendment, "suffrage women retreated into their own special interests, organizations, and regional concerns, often taking opposing sides on policy issues."[5] Both the National American Woman Suffrage Association (NAWSA) and the NWP looked toward their respective futures. Earlier that year, NAWSA reorganized as the League of Women Voters of the United States (LWVUS) and thus began their "mighty political experiment" to educate and register women to vote. Within just a few years, the league's work expanded significantly, and they launched their first "Get Out the Vote" campaign.[6] The NWP chose neither to participate in voter education programs nor accept the invitation to join Black women's efforts to fight against Jim Crow laws and lynching. Instead, the NWP shifted focus to their new legislative effort—the ERA.[7]

After the Nineteenth Amendment, the major racial divisions that had fractured suffrage organizations reemerged in women's political advocacy groups. Black women who faced both gender barriers and racial discrimination were once again excluded by the predominantly White organizations, so they continued their independent efforts toward political equality and social reform by resuming their work through Black churches, clubs, and academic institutions. Sororities, for example, played a critical role in these efforts. Historian Paula Giddings writes, "The sorority has always been an important source of leadership training for Black women, whose opportunities to exercise such skills in formal organizations are few."[8] Zeta Phi Beta was founded in 1920 specifically to support social causes important to the Black community. Women also joined the Alpha Kappa Alpha Sorority and the Delta Sigma Theta Sorority—both founded at Howard University, in 1908 and 1913, respectively. In 1922 Sigma Gamma Rho joined the original three as the sorority for Black professional teachers.[9] These four early sororities became one of the building blocks for promoting education and civic engagement within African American communities. Krysta Jones, a political advisor, notes that even today sororities continue to be "a large part of Black social and community life."[10]

The limitations of the Nineteenth Amendment as well as new discriminatory legislation enacted within the following decades influenced many people, including Native American women. In 1924 the Indian Citizenship Act was passed, which held that all Native

Americans born in the United States were citizens; however, it left the decision of who could legally vote up to the states, opening the door for disenfranchisement.[11] By 1928, the Arizona Supreme Court ruled that Native Americans were wards of the government and therefore ineligible to vote. More than thirty years passed before Native Americans living on reservations in New Mexico, Arizona, Utah, and North Dakota litigated to reinstate their voting rights; nonetheless, voter-suppression tactics such as literacy tests remained in place in Arizona until 1970.[12]

Despite the Nineteenth Amendment, efforts to suppress voters in the following decades also kept some immigrants, Hispanics, and Asian Americans—women and men—away from the voting booth. The inherent language barriers were exacerbated by poll taxes and literacy tests as well as uncertainty around voting locations.[13] By 1929 the three major Mexican American organizations joined forces to create the League of United Latin American Citizens (LULAC), which at the time became the largest civil rights organization for Mexican Americans.[14] The ongoing voter suppression of Asian immigrants and Asian Americans began with efforts to prevent them from becoming American citizens. Seen as "perpetual

Figure 3.1. Smith, Roger, photographer. Washington, D.C. Mary McLeod Bethune at Phyllis Wheatley YWCA Young Women's Christian Association on Rhode Island Avenue. United States Washington D.C. District of Columbia Washington D.C., 1943. July. Photograph. https://www.loc .gov/item/2017859749/. Library of Congress, Prints & Photographs Division, Farm Security Administration/Office of War Information Black-and-White Negatives

foreigners," the ongoing discriminative laws and practices forbade them from owning property, becoming naturalized citizens, and registering to vote.[15]

Amid the continued battles over enfranchisement after the Nineteenth Amendment, the country faced immense economic challenges. The stock market crash of 1929 led to widespread unemployment and poverty and ushered in the Great Depression. Farmers and consumers began to default on loans, which further destabilized the banking industry. Herbert Hoover lost the presidential election of 1932, as the country voted instead for Franklin Delano Roosevelt and his economic recovery plan—the New Deal. While the legislation did not include a civil rights component for African Americans, there was an indirect benefit, as Roosevelt appointed Mary McLeod Bethune as the director of negro affairs of the National Youth Administration. Bethune, along with other high-level African American appointees, formed a "kitchen cabinet" that had direct access to the president. By 1936 African American voters had shifted their support to the Democratic Party.[16] The continued fight to expand enfranchisement, coupled with the decade-long economic downturn, influenced the way that the country would memorialize the Nineteenth Amendment's twenty-fifth anniversary in 1945. However, this milestone was most profoundly shaped by the country's involvement in World War II.

The Twenty-Fifth Anniversary (1945): Overshadowed by War

The United States entered World War II in December 1941 after the attack on the naval base and headquarters of the U.S. Pacific Fleet at Pearl Harbor. Thus, the primary focus of the country at the time pivoted toward uniting Americans together against a common wartime enemy. Four years later, the twenty-fifth anniversary recognizing the passage of the Nineteenth Amendment did not receive much public attention at the national level. President Harry S. Truman offered a measured statement recognizing the anniversary, "It is fitting that we, men and women alike, should give thanks for an America in which women can stand on the level footing of full citizenship in peace and in war."[17] Given the upheaval of the preceding four years, it is not surprising that the anniversary did not garner widespread notice.

Although few public celebrations took place, the small town of Rochester, New York, marked the anniversary with a public jubilee in honor of local citizen Susan B. Anthony. In 1865 Anthony and her family had rented a home on Madison Street, where she would live until her death in 1906. In 1945 after a multi-year effort, the Rochester Federation of Women's Clubs raised the necessary $8,500 to purchase the house in order to "preserve the home of one of the great women of our country and so keep her memory green and her ideals before us."[18] The local community gathered to celebrate Anthony's work for enfranchisement and opened her house as a museum.

In hindsight, it is clear that the important economic, political, and social events of the events leading up to 1945 had a significant impact on the first celebration. As we turn our focus to subsequent anniversaries, we will see familiar challenges such as shifting cultural and economic patterns and political strife leading up to the events recognizing the fiftieth anniversary of the ratification of the Nineteenth Amendment.

The Fiftieth Anniversary (1970): A Call to Action

In the years between 1945 and 1970, women's political and civic activism, along with demands for equality under the law, continued; however, social, political, and cultural shifts continued to limit women's progress toward achieving equality. In postwar America, the rise of the middle class and their important role as consumers was widely heralded in popular magazines such as *Good Housekeeping* and the *Ladies Home Journal*, both focused primarily on the domesticity of White, middle-class women. In another example, the *Chicago Defender*—a prominent African American newspaper known for covering anti-lynching efforts, race riots, and the Great Migration—hosted a major housewares show in fall of 1959 that highlighted Black businesses alongside national brands like Whirlpool.[19] Taken together, it is clear that all three publications recognized the economic importance of the middle-class consumer. However, many women—including women of color, who were already in the workforce, though mainly as domestic, low-wage, and part-time hourly workers, as well as White women, who had joined the workforce for the first time—were left out of the 1950s image of the middle-class American housewife.[20]

Throughout these decades, civil rights activists continued to challenge White supremacy through mobilizing and organizing within their communities. These efforts in part ushered in major political and cultural shifts, including the end to legal segregation practices in public spaces and schools.[21] Black women from all walks of life played instrumental roles in this work. For example, Septima Clark started citizenship schools; Fannie Lou Hamer pushed to register voters and co-founded the Mississippi Freedom Democratic Party; and Jo Ann Robinson, who was active in the Women's Political Council, fought for desegregation most notably on the Montgomery Bus Boycott.[22]

Hispanic Americans and Asian Americans also expanded their efforts to press for voting rights and civil rights. Caesar Chavez, Delores Huerta, and Gilbert Padilla established the United Farm Workers of America in 1962 to improve living and working conditions for agricultural farm workers.[23] Others sought to build on the work of the LULAC, including the Viva Kennedy club in Texas. Later the Mexican American Legal Defense Fund formed in the late 1960s.[24] Asian American communities continued to fight; while the passage of the Immigration and Nationality Act of 1965 reduced decades of restrictive immigration policies, there was still work to be done.[25] The Asian American Political Alliance formed at University of California at Berkeley and worked to unite all Asian Americans and work together for social change.[26]

In 1963 President John F. Kennedy was assassinated. However, the civil rights and voting rights activists around the country had already laid the groundwork for Lyndon B. Johnson to usher in the Civil Rights Act in 1964 and the Voting Rights Act of 1965. The ongoing work by women's rights activists had also compelled Kennedy to establish the President's Commission on the Status of Women, which "set the stage for the emergence of liberal feminism in the mid-to-late 1960s."[27] By 1963 Betty Friedan had published her groundbreaking work, *The Feminine Mystique*, which countered the popular idea that women could only find fulfillment through childbearing and homemaking.

While progress toward women's political equality had been made in the fifty years since the ratification of the Nineteenth Amendment, many women still felt undervalued both in the workplace and at home. Furthermore, women were still being denied basic rights that would be considered simple liberties in twenty-first-century American society. For example, single women could not legally access birth control, and financial institutions and department stores would not issue a credit card or bank loan to a married woman in her own name. It was also still standard employment practice for job postings to be listed under "Help Wanted—Male and Help Wanted—Female."[28] Unfortunately before the decade would end, both Dr. Martin Luther King Jr. and Bobby F. Kennedy would also be assassinated, bringing the tumultuous decade to a close.

Figure 3.2. Leffler, Warren K, photographer. Civil rights march on Washington, D.C. / WKL. Washington D.C., 1963. Photograph. https://www.loc.gov/item/2003654393/. Library of Congress, Prints and Photographs Division, U.S. News & World Report Magazine Photograph Collection

And so, on the eve of the fiftieth anniversary of the ratification of the Nineteenth Amendment, tens of thousands of American women were not just preparing to celebrate the opportunities that enfranchisement had provided but also organizing a nationwide strike to demand an expansion of their existing rights and privileges.[29] The Women's Strike for Equality along with protest rallies, "teach-ins," and "sit-ins"—all tactics learned from the Black Civil Rights Movement—took place on August 26, 1970, in New York City. Sources estimated that as many as ten thousand women marched down Fifth Avenue and then rallied in Bryant Park to raise awareness and fight for what they saw as fundamental rights for women.[30] Many protesters demanded access to abortion services and birth control, the establishment of community-controlled and around-the-clock daycare centers for the children of working mothers, and equal access to education and employment opportunities for women.[31]

As part of the anniversary, women of all ages, as well as many male supporters, marched in at least fifty other cities across the country. Estimates for the "sister marches" held in Detroit, Minneapolis, Berkeley, New Orleans, Boston, Chicago, and Indianapolis numbered between ten thousand and twenty thousand participants.[32] The National Organization for Women (NOW) acted as the primary organizer of the 1970 Women's Strike for Equality.[33] Pauli Murray, who along with Betty Friedan co-founded NOW in 1966, played a prominent role. Eleanor Holmes Norton, who at the time served as chair of New York City's Commission on Human Rights, as well as activist Bella Abzug, also participated in the activities (Abzug and Norton would later serve in the U.S. House of Representatives).[34]

By 1970 the ERA, which by then had languished in congressional committee for forty-seven years, was now once again seen as a priority for a new generation of women who stood ready to demand their rights.[35] However, the feminist platform did not appeal to all women; there were those who believed that the ERA would bring an unwelcomed impact and even disruption to their lives, and so they were against it.[36]

When looking back at the events unfolding at this time, we need to ask critical questions: Who was excluded from the women's movement of the 1960s and 1970s, and why? Certainly some women were simply uninterested and therefore chose not to participate.

Figure 3.3. Leffler, Warren K, photographer. Demonstrators opposed to the ERA in front of the White House. Washington D.C., 1977. Feb. 4. Photograph. https://www.loc.gov/item/2002712194/. Library of Congress, Prints and Photographs Division, U.S. News & World Report Magazine Photograph Collection

However, others were excluded based on their ethnicity, economic status, or sexual preference. Lesbians and bisexuals who were initially attracted to the feminist movement, for example, were sometimes excluded from participating alongside heterosexual women. At this time the gay liberation movement (as it was called in the early 1970s) was still largely unrecognized by the general public, as the Stonewall riots in New York City had only taken place in 1969.[37] Due to this, many activists within the lesbian and bisexual communities moved on and formed their own organizations with their own unique political demands, one of the largest being the African American lesbian feminist organization the Combahee River Collective out of Boston.[38]

The Seventy-Fifth Anniversary (1995): Using a Historic Lens

The establishment and expansion of women's history as an academic discipline in the late twentieth century significantly influenced the programmatic content of the seventy-fifth anniversary. By the 1970s, a burgeoning interest in women's history had prompted scholars and practitioners to examine women's efforts to obtain political, social, and economic rights in the United States. The recognition of women's history as a valid pursuit of academic inquiry resulted in efforts to amplify and commemorate the historic women's rights

Figure 3.4. Seventy-fifth anniversary edition of the National Women's History Project "Women Win the Vote." Image courtesy of Robert Cooney

movement.[39] In 1971, Bella Abzug introduced legislation to officially recognize August 26 as Women's Equality Day, which Congress passed.[40] By 1980, the newly founded National Women's History Project (NWHP) began lobbying for the designation of the first week in March to be recognized as Women's History Week.[41] President Jimmy Carter, by proclamation, made the designation and simultaneously called for the ratification of the proposed Twenty-Seventh Amendment, the ERA.[42] The NWHP continued their push, and in 1987 they successfully extended the one-week commemoration to the full month of March, which is still widely recognized today.[43]

However, in contrast, the 1980s also ushered in a return to conservatism with the election of popular-actor-turned-politician Ronald Reagan, and all the while younger women were increasingly not self-identifying as feminists in comparison to the generation before them.[44] Sexist and racist actions continued to complicate women's lives; one notable example was the Supreme Court confirmation process for Judge Clarence Thomas in 1991 when Anita Hill accused the nominee, her supervisor at the U.S. Department of Education and the Equal Employment Opportunity Commission, of sexual harassment. Even so, women made substantial political gains. The congressional hearings and press coverage documenting Thomas's ultimate confirmation to the Supreme Court despite Anita Hill's accusations of sexual harassment invigorated public debate on women's equality. Subsequently, twenty-three women were elected to the U.S. House and U.S. Senate in the 103rd Congress. Given this, 1992 was later dubbed the "Year of the Woman."[45]

Celebrations for the seventy-fifth anniversary focused largely on recognizing those who were on the frontlines of the work for enfranchisement in the early twentieth century. Due to this, the anniversary programs in 1995 largely overlooked the post-suffrage women and organizations that continued and expanded the work toward equality from the 1920s and later.[46] Notably this included more recent organizations such as the Third World Women's Alliance, which grew out of Student Non-Violent Coordinator Committee. The Black Women's Liberation Committee, which focused on Cuba; the Comisión Femenil Mexicana Nacional, which focused on the needs of Chicanas worldwide; and Asian Women United, which worked to expose and eliminate racist and sexist views were largely omitted.[47]

The seventy-fifth anniversary events included a series of lectures, museum exhibits, and a Women's Rights Forum that focused largely on celebrating the historic significance of the suffrage movement and the key figures, largely White women, within it. While small-scale public events took place in communities across the country, the national spotlight focused on programs held at multiple locations in Washington, DC. The National Archives Records Administration commissioned the original play *Failure Is Impossible* and hosted a program featuring dramatic readings and attended by high-profile guests such as author Cokie Roberts and former congresswoman and civil rights icon Barbara Jordan.[48] The Women's Suffrage Anniversary Task Force, working under the auspices of the NWP, promoted an afternoon rally on the National Mall promoting women's equality as part of the memorialization efforts. In addition, the Smithsonian National Museum of American History hosted a history symposium that was moderated by Marjorie Spruill. Additionally, Supreme Court Justice Sandra Day O'Connor headlined a political forum by the League of Women Voters. The commemorative events extended into September with the temporary display of the original Nineteenth Amendment at the U.S. Capitol.[49]

VOTES FOR WOMEN

★ ★ ★ ★ ★

Visions of Equality
Past and Future

A Symposium Celebrating
the 75th Anniversary
of Woman Suffrage

Sponsored by
National Museum of American History
National Museum of Women in the Arts
75th Anniversary of Woman Suffrage Task Force

August 25, 1995 ★ 8:45 a.m.–5:15 p.m.
National Museum of American History
Smithsonian Institution

Figure 3.5.   Cover of the program for "Visions of Equality: Past and Future,"
a symposium sponsored in part by the National Museum of American
History in celebration of the seventy-fifth anniversary of women's suffrage.
Image courtesy of Robert Cooney

By 1995, scholars and practitioners had begun to address the enduring pattern of omitting the contributions of women of color to both the historic suffrage movement and second-wave feminism. Even so, looking back at the programmatic content and offerings through a twenty-first-century lens, it is clear that events were neither equal nor inclusive for women of color. Only a few African American women such as Sojourner Truth, Ida B. Wells-Barnett, and Mary Church Terrell were regularly highlighted.

Nonetheless, some individual scholars and institutions were working to amplify the role of women of color in these movements and to address the racist practices that contributed to their omission in the first place.[50] One such example is Marjorie Spruill's *One Woman, One Vote: Rediscovering the Woman Suffrage Movement*, which remains a valuable resource for public historians and practitioners. Written as a companion book to augment the *One Woman, One Vote* video produced by the Educational Film Center (ELC) for the PBS series "American Experience" and funded by National Endowment for the Humanities, it shares valuable content and also features a diverse range of women's history scholars.[51]

Spruill's book chronicles the abolition movement, Reconstruction legislation including the Fourteenth and Fifteenth Amendments to the Constitution, the reconciliation of the two major organizations working for suffrage, and the connection between abolition and temperance. Essays by Ellen Carol DuBois outline the economic issues and class divisions within the suffrage movement.[52] Rosalyn Terborg-Penn, Wanda Hendricks, and Beverly Beeton highlight the contributions and leadership of African American women in the suffrage, abolition, and temperance movements. Additional essays add rich content around questions of citizenship that impacted Native Americans, Asian Americans, and Indigenous peoples.[53]

In contrast, the *One Woman, One Vote* video content falls noticeably short; the section highlighting the contributions of African American women is not introduced until over thirty minutes into the almost-two-hour-long piece, and the segment itself lasts just under five minutes. Additionally, out of the twelve scholars featured on camera, only one woman of color is included. Terborg-Penn speaks candidly and unapologetically while addressing racism within the suffrage movement and quickly dispels the idea that political expediency alone allowed the practice to continue. In one particularly powerful segment, Terborg-Penn chronicles how the organizational strategies by suffrage leaders of the largest organizations, such as the NWP and NAWSA, sympathized with the southern states and, in doing so, contributed to the rise of Jim Crow discrimination efforts against women's enfranchisement. She notes that voting rights for African American women were more important than just an act of civic engagement; for them, it was "a question of life or death."[54] When comparing the book to the video, the former is a far better example of a thoroughly inclusive resource, and as such remains relevant today. An updated and expanded edition of *One Woman, One Vote* will be published in 2021.

Learning from Our History

The racist practice of erasing women of color from the historical narrative is one that is deeply rooted in women's history. Lisa Tetrault reminds us in *The Myth of Seneca Falls* that in one of the first accounts of the early suffrage movement, the multi-volume *History of Woman Suffrage*, Sojourner Truth is reduced to a "supporting cast member, not a main figure" by authors Susan B. Anthony and Elizabeth Cady Stanton.[55] This practice of reducing the actions, voices, and intent of women of color will continue unless there is a concerted effort by practitioners, scholars, and educators working collectively and proactively to correct it.

Looking back, we see that the ebb and flow of the political rhetoric and cultural dialogue that guided the recognition efforts of the twenty-fifth, fiftieth, and the seventy-fifth anniversaries greatly influenced the content of programs and events. By 1995 work to include an inclusive narrative was underway and more women of color were featured at events and in the media. Nonetheless, the work of White historians and activists continued to dominate the field. As we continue to explore, develop, and produce public programs at museums and historic sites, we must continue to expand the narrative of women's enfranchisement to include voting rights, civil rights, and citizenship. Our actions will serve to expand the relevance of the history, not only for younger generations to whom this is a new story, but also for those who have not previously seen themselves reflected in the historic interpretations of the past. It is time to learn from past mistakes, correct the inaccuracies, and expand our interpretation of the women's suffrage movement.

Notes

1. Seth Bruggeman, "Introduction: Conundrum and Nuance in American Memory," in *Commemoration: The American Association for State and Local History Guide*, ed. Seth C. Bruggeman (Lanham, MD: Rowman & Littlefield, 2017), 7.
2. The activities around the centennial in 2020 are included in chapter 11.
3. For more information, see Hasan Kwame Jeffries, ed., *Understanding and Teaching the Civil Rights Movement* (Madison: University of Wisconsin Press, 2019); Lorraine Gates Schuyler, *The Weight of Their Votes: Southern Women and Political Leverage in the 1920s* (Chapel Hill, University of North Carolina Press, 2006); and Glenda Elizabeth Gilmore, *Gender & Jim Crow: Women and Politics of White Supremacy in North Carolina, 1896–1920* (Chapel Hill: University of North Carolina Press, 1996).
4. Schuyler, *The Weight of Their Votes*, 51–52.
5. Elaine Weiss, *The Woman's Hour: The Great Fight to Win the Vote* (New York: Viking Press, 2018), 332.
6. Barbara Stuhler, *For the Public Record: A Documentary History of the League of Women Voters* (Westport, CT: Greenwood Press, 2000).
7. Leila J. Rupp and Verta A. Taylor, *Survival in the Doldrums: The American Women's Rights Movement, 1945 to the 1960s* (Columbus: Ohio State University Press, 1990), 25.
8. Paula Giddings, *In Search of Sisterhood: Delta Sigma Theta and the Challenge of the Black Sorority Movement* (New York: Amistad, 1988), 16.
9. "The Divine Nine and the National Pan-Hellenic Council," accessed September 2019, www .blackgreek.com/divinenine.
10. Krysta Jones, email correspondence with author, January–March 2019. Krysta Jones speaks frequently about how being part of the Zeta Phi Beta Sorority has impacted her personally, and she acknowledges that her sorority sisters gave her a sense of community and a support network that she still relies on.
11. The Indian Citizenship Act of 1924, Pub. L. No. 68-175, 43 Stat 253 (1924).
12. "Fighting for a Voice: Native Americans' Right to Vote in Arizona," Arizona Historical Society, July 15, 2020, https://arizonahistoricalsociety.org/2020/07/15/fighting-for-a-voice -native-americans-right-to-vote-in-arizona; and Patty Ferguson-Bohnee, "How the Native American Vote Continues to Be Suppressed," www.americanbar.org/groups/crsj/publications/

human_rights_magazine_home/voting-rights/how-the-native-american-vote-continues-to
-be-suppressed.

13. Susan Cianci Salvatore, ed., *Civil Rights in America: Racial Voting Rights, a National Historic Landmarks Theme Study*, rev. ed. (Washington, DC: National Park Service, 2009), 8, www.nps .gov/subjects/tellingallamericansstories/upload/CivilRights_VotingRights.pdf.

14. "LULAC History—All for One and One for All," League of United Latin American Citizens, accessed June 2019, https://lulac.org/about/history.

15. Japanese American Citizens League, *An Unnoticed Struggle: A Concise History of Asian American Civil Rights Issues*, 2008, https://jacl.org/wordpress/wp-content/uploads/2015/01/Unnoticed-Struggle.pdf.

16. Salvatore, *Civil Rights in America*, 19.

17. Harry S. Truman, "Statement by the President on the 25th Anniversary of the Women's Suffrage Amendment," August 25, 1945, Harry S. Truman Papers, Secretary Papers, Harry S. Truman Library and Museum, www.trumanlibrary.gov/library/public-papers/111/statement -president-25th-anniversary-womens-suffrage-amendment.

18. Mrs. George Howard, "19th Amendment Jubilee Sunday Should See Anthony Quota," *Rochester (NY) Democrat and Chronicle*, August 19, 1945.

19. Adrienne Samuels Gibbs, "How the Obsidian Collection Is Bringing Black Newspapers to Google," *Chicago*, June 4, 2018, www.chicagomag.com/city-life/June-2018/How-the-Obsidian -Collection-Is-Bringing-Black-Newspapers-to-Google.

20. Kirsten Swinth, *Feminism's Forgotten Fight: The Unfinished Struggle for Work and Family* (Cambridge, MA: Harvard University Press, 2018), 2–6, 76–77.

21. Jeffries, *Understanding and Teaching the Civil Rights Movement*, 86–89.

22. Salvatore, *Civil Rights in America*, 42, 59–60.

23. National Park Service, *American Latinos and the Making of the United States: A Theme Study*, 2013, www.nps.gov/heritageinitiatives/latino/latinothemestudy.

24. Victoria-Maria McDonald, "Demanding Their Rights: The Latino Struggle for Educational Access and Equity," *American Latinos and the Making of the United States: A Theme Study*, National Park Service, 2013, www.nps.gov/heritageinitiatives/latino/latinothemestudy/pdfs/ Education_final_web.pdf.

25. C. N. Le, "The 1965 Immigration Act," Asian Nation: The Landscape of Asian America, January 27, 2021, www.asian-nation.org/1965-immigration-act.shtml#sthash.r8yYWODB .dpbs.

26. https://jacl.org/wordpress/wp-content/uploads/2015/01/Unnoticed-Struggle.pdf.

27. Elizabeth Singer More, "Report of the President's Commission on the Status of Women: Background, Content, Significance," Harvard University, accessed June 2019, www.radcliffe .harvard.edu/sites/default/files/documents/report_of_the_presidents_commission_on_the_ status_of_women_background_content_significance.pdf.

28. Cheri Register, "When Women Went Public: Feminist Reforms in the 1970s," *Minnesota History* 61, no. 2 (Summer 2008): 62.

29. Marjorie J. Spruill. *Divided We Stand: The Battle Over Women's Rights and Family Values That Polarized American Politics* (New York: Bloomsbury, 2017), 24.

30. Linda Charlton, "Women Marched Down Fifth in Equality Drive," *New York Times*, August 27, 1970.

31. Charlton, "Women Marched Down Fifth."

32. Based on the numbers cited in sister marches in Charlton, "Women Marched Down Fifth." Register, "When Women Went Public."

33. Spruill, *Divided We Stand*, 24.

34. Eleanor Holmes Norton has served as a non-voting delegate representing the District of Columbia since 1990. For more information, see Norton's congressional website, https://norton .house.gov. Bella Abzug served from 1971 through 1978 representing the state of New York; for more information, see "Abzug, Bella Savitzky," History, Art, and Archives, U.S. House of Representatives, accessed September 2, 2020, https://history.house.gov/People/Detail/8276.

35. Jo Freeman, "Political Organization in the Feminist Movement," *Acta Sociologica* 18, no. 2–3, (1975): 222–28.

36. Spruill, *Divided We Stand*, 12.

37. Susan Ferentinos, *Interpreting LGBT History at Museums and Historic Sites* (Lanham, MD: Rowman & Littlefield, 2015), 83.

38. Ferentinos, *Interpreting LGBT History*, 82.

39. At this time, women did work to claim public spaces in which they could educate themselves, spaces that were filled with books written for women and by women. The NWP opened the Florence Bayard Hilles Feminist Library at their headquarters on Capitol Hill in Washington, DC. They believed that by providing "resources to women about their own history as well as opportunities to join the movement for equal rights across the country and throughout the world" would have a broad and lasting benefit for all women. The Schlesinger Library at Radcliffe, now known as one of the foremost libraries on women's history in the United States, began with the initial donation of Maud Wood Park's suffrage papers. These libraries, both founded in 1943, are still valuable resources for public historians of women's history and scholars today.

40. Eliza Berman, "Meet the Woman Behind Women's Equality Day," *Time,* August 26, 2016.

41. Founded by Molly Murphy MacGregor, Mary Ruthsdotter, Maria Cuevas, Paula Hammett, and Bette Morgan. "Our History," National Women's History Alliance, accessed July 8, 2020, www.nwhp.org/about-2/our-history.

42. Jimmy Carter, "National Women's History Week Statement by the President," February 28, 1980, American Presidency Project, www.presidency.ucsb.edu/documents/national-womens -history-week-statement-the-president.

43. "Our History," National Women's History Alliance, 2018.

44. Spruill, *Divided We Stand*, 31.

45. "The Year of the Woman," History, Art and Archives, U.S. House of Representatives, accessed September 3, 2020, https://history.house.gov/Exhibitions-and-Publications/WIC/Historical -Essays/Assembling-Amplifying-Ascending/Women-Decade.

46. There are many notable examples of scholarship from the timeframe and later; for more information, see Daina Ramey Berry and Kali Nicole Gross, *A Black Women's History of the United States* (Boston: Beacon Press, 2020); Irma McClaurin, ed. *Black Feminist Anthropology: Theory, Politics, Praxis, and Poetics* (New Brunswick, NJ: Rutgers University Press, 2001); Ellen Carol DuBois and Vicki L. Ruiz, eds., *Unequal Sisters: A Multi-Cultural Reader in U.S. Women's History* (New York: Routledge, 1990); Cherrie Moraga and Gloria Anzaldua, eds., *This Bridge Called My Back: Writings by Radical Women of Color* (Watertown, MA: Persephone Press, 1981); and Daisy Hernandez and Bushra Rehman, eds., *Colorize This!: Young Women of Color on Today's Feminism* (Berkeley: Seal Press, 2002).

47. Ashley Farmer, "The Third World Women's Alliance, Cuba, and the Exchange of Ideas," Black Perspectives, April 7, 2017, www.aaihs.org/the-third-world-womens-alliance-cuba-and-the-exchange-of-ideas; and "Comisión Femenil Mexicana Nacional, Inc," University of California Santa Barbara Library, accessed December 2020, www.library.ucsb.edu/special-collections/cema/cfmn.

48. Rosemary H. Knower, "Failure is Impossible," Educator Resources, National Archives Records Administration, accessed July 10, 2020, www.archives.gov/education/lessons/woman-suffrage/script.html.

49. Holly Bass, "75th Anniversary of Women's Suffrage," *Washington City Paper*, August 26, 1995.

50. Sandra Weber, *The Woman Suffrage Statue: A History of Adelaide Johnson's Portrait Monument at the United States Capitol* (Jefferson, NC: McFarland, 2016), 188.

51. Ruth Pollack, *One Woman, One Vote*, PBS, 1995, DVD.

52. Ellen Carol DuBois, "Working Women, Class Relations, and Suffrage Militance: Harriot Stanton Blatch and the New York Woman Suffrage Movement," in *One Woman, One Vote: Rediscovering the Woman Suffrage Movement,* ed. Marjorie Julian Spruill (Troutdale, OR: NewSage Press, 1995), 221–44.

53. Rosalyn Terborg-Penn, "African American Women and the Woman Suffrage Movement," in Spruill, *One Woman, One Vote*, 138; Wanda Hendricks, "Ida B. Wells-Barnett and the Alpha Suffrage Club of Chicago," in Spruill, *One Woman, One Vote*, 267–76; Beverly Beeton, "How the West Was Won For Suffrage," in Spruill, *One Woman, One Vote*, 99–116.

54. Terborg-Penn, "African American Women and the Woman Suffrage Movement," in Pollack, *One Woman, One Vote.*

55. Lisa Tetrault, *The Myth of Seneca Falls: Memory and the Women's Suffrage Movement, 1848–1898* (Chapel Hill: University of North Carolina Press, 2014), 134.

CHAPTER 4

Revealing Racism in Women's Suffrage

OUR WORK TO EXPLORE ALL ASPECTS OF THE HISTORY of women's political activism including racism is vital. However, some organizations resist even acknowledging this history because doing so can create a negative public image, which then has the potential to alienate visitors, stakeholders, and donors. To overcome this challenge, we must do the initial work to develop strategies that build strong systems of internal and external support so that undertaking difficult projects is possible. Ultimately each museum and historic site will find a distinct way to accomplish their work; however, reviewing the efforts of our fellow history practitioners as they work to reveal the role of racism within their own historic sites and organizations is a good place to start.

In the following chapters, we will examine the work at three women's history sites to correct gaps in their historical interpretations prompted by unacknowledged racism within their institutions. The goal in sharing these case studies is twofold: first, to examine and chronicle ongoing efforts to repair the damage previously inflicted through racially insensitive methods of interpretation; and second, to disseminate information throughout the field and encourage similar efforts at other historic sites and museums. To be clear, the purpose is not to judge or label work at these sites as either a "success" or "failure." Instead, it is to review their progress so that we may understand the difficulties in attempting and executing this type of work as well as to generate ideas that will help us navigate the common barriers we face as a field.

The General Federation of Women's Clubs (GFWC), the NWP, and the Frances Willard House Museum (FWHM) are all in varying states of addressing racial bias and systemic racism within their own histories. All three are nationally recognized women's organizations that were founded more than one hundred years ago. Unfortunately, members and leaders of all three organizations have condoned and even engaged in racist behavior that has contributed to the marginalization of women of color, and coming to terms with this history remains a struggle.

The General Federation of Women's Clubs

Founded in 1890, the GFWC has operated from their headquarters at 1734 N Street NW in Washington, DC, since 1922. The headquarters, a National Historic Landmark, does not function as a museum, per se; however, staff highlights the GFWC's history through tours of the site, public programs, and online exhibits. The Women's History and Resource Center (WHRC) is a publicly accessible archive within the headquarters that maintains a collection of approximately ten thousand objects and archival records. With over three hundred linear feet of processed records, the GFWC's archives focus primarily on the national level of the federation and capture community life from 1890 to the present. The GFWC also maintains an oral history collection of more than four hundred interviews that document the lives and contributions of clubwomen throughout the twentieth century.[1] The GFWC has one full-time archivist who also acts as the manager of the WHRC.

Like other women's organizations of the time, the GFWC has a history that is complicated by the unaddressed racism within their history. As shown in the case study offered by Alyssa Constad, early membership in the GFWC consisted mainly of "wealthy, socially elite, white women, [who were] moved to promote public education, child labor laws, environmental regulation, and other issues which fit into the package of domestic feminism." Despite their seemingly progressive agenda, serious inconsistencies emerge when viewing the GFWC through a modern lens such as their refusal to formally support women's suffrage until 1914. In addition, Black women were not given the opportunity to participate nor rise to leadership positions within the organization in the same ways as White women.

As an institution, the GFWC has yet to formally delve into and facilitate a dialogue around the more controversial aspects of their history. Ample documentation of these racial tensions exists in the archives, though it is unlikely that GFWC leadership will deem it a priority to address them in the near future. In order for their case study to be included in this volume, GFWC staff engaged board leadership in lengthy discussions. Ultimately, the executive committee gave their permission—a small but important first step. As such, the GFWC has made a tacit attempt to begin a much-needed conversation. That said, if a deep analysis of the historical facts is to be done, it will more than likely be led by external sources within the field of women's history or another academic discipline. And while it may be difficult for contemporary audiences to reconcile the contradictory nature of the organization today, the GFWC was, and is, hardly alone in their reticence to address issues of race and racism among their members.

The National Woman's Party

Founded by Alice Paul in final years before the ratification of the Nineteenth Amendment, the NWP continued their work for women's equality by supporting the ERA well into the early 1990s. By 1997 they ceased their lobbying efforts and concentrated on running the SBHM as a public museum. Their historical interpretation, however, focused almost exclusively on telling the story of women's history through the lens of predominantly White, middle- to upper-class women. In addition to exhibits, the museum has convened panel discussions and public programs about issues important to women. The archive of the NWP remains on-site and holds almost one thousand banners, sashes, and other textiles from the suffrage and ERA campaigns.

In her case study, Jennifer Krafchik highlights the multiple attempts to explore the more troubling aspects of racism that existed within the ranks of the NWP. For many years, the primary narrative has featured the efforts of White activists picketing the White House, marching in parades, and participating in other public events. This limited narrative has remained generally unquestioned by the public and applauded by visitors, donors, and board members. Though the historic narrative should indeed showcase the bold actions and efforts by White suffragists in the face of both physical danger and public ridicule, making it the singular focus has allowed racism within the suffrage movement to remain hidden.

There is no doubt that efforts in the last twenty years have steered the SBHM's historical narrative toward a more honest and inclusive storyline. Unfortunately, this work has often been undermined by the institution's serious financial instability, which is typical of small public history sites. As a result, the leadership focused on shoring up financial shortfalls, which often correlated to cuts in programming, exhibits, and even staff. The case study shows how a major reinterpretation project such as this can take years and, in this instance, last for well over a decade. Now that NPS operates the SBHM, work on a new interpretation plan that further explores biases and racism is underway.

Frances Willard House Museum

One of the earliest historic sites named for a woman, the Frances Willard House opened as a public museum in 1900, just two years after Willard's death. The museum offers public tours and programming around women's leadership, higher education, social reform movements, temperance, and prohibition. Additionally, Willard's personal papers and the organizational records of the Woman's Christian Temperance Union (WCTU) are archived on-site and available to the public.

Under the leadership of museum director Lori Osborne, the FWHM has closely examined the public and contentious conflict between Frances Willard and Ida B. Wells that played out in early twentieth-century newspapers. Their conflict began with Willard's racist comments during an interview, which Wells deemed were in conflict with Willard's international reputation as a Christian reformer. Willard also refused to publicly support Wells's work on anti-lynching campaigns, which allowed their public animosity to grow.

Coming to terms with Willard's limited perspective—particularly around race and identity—and her propensity to use racial stereotypes to forward the WCTU's agenda is a challenging endeavor. When discussing the FWHM's ongoing work, Osborne states, "This exploration has been difficult, but it has been more than worth the time and effort. And really, that is why we are doing this project—to do this hard work ourselves and to encourage others to do so. It is so needed."[2] The FWHM has boldly stepped away from solely interpreting Frances Willard's story and instead has fostered a more public-led historical inquiry, which has allowed visitors and the community to provide feedback. Of the three sites, the FWHM is arguably the furthest along in making the necessary changes to address the racial discrimination in their history. Osborne's case study outlines the "Truth-Telling Project" along with the www.willardandwells.org documentary website and digital repository.

Taking Action to Confront Racism

As a former executive director of the SBHM, I can attest to the difficult nature of confronting a historic narrative that includes biases and racism. Furthermore, I admit that my reticence to making necessary changes hindered the progress toward acknowledging racism within the NWP. Together, these case studies reveal that substantive progress only begins once an organization fully commits to taking action. This commitment can be broken down into three initial steps: First, an organization must undertake an internal examination and make a decision to move forward. Second, they need to resolve to expand their community base. Finally, staff, board members, and stakeholders must take a leap of faith by moving forward, even without a clear understanding of where the process will lead.

The internal examination is critical, as it sets the stage for the rest of the work. Engaging in conversations that go beyond a superficial analysis of racism is something that each of the three organizations has struggled with at both the board and staff levels. That said, the aversion to confronting racism within predominantly White organizations is not unique to the GFWC, NWP, and FWHM; it is evident at museums and historic sites of all types and sizes. When we use author and educator Robin DiAngelo's lens of "white fragility" to evaluate each organization, we recognize that a common thread linking the case studies is the tendency to reduce "racism to a matter of nice people versus mean people."[3] Given that the women who founded and worked for each organization have been lauded as icons, it is problematic to describe them as anything less than perfect.

Even without applying the incendiary label of "racist" to an individual, it can still be controversial even to describe the actions of a historic figure as "racially biased." For example, if we characterize Alice Paul and the other NWP leaders' actions in expecting Black women to march at the back of the 1913 Woman's Suffrage Procession as racially motivated, does this mean that these female icons were racist, biased, or simply flawed? Does the answer change when we take into consideration that at the time, racial segregation in public was still legal and culturally acceptable? And a bigger question remains: Does a label that is applied one hundred years after the fact erase the many years of work, personal sacrifice, and positive actions by the suffragists that improved the lives of so many women?

These are critical questions that deserve thoughtful answers, but first we must go beyond applying binary labels that divide historic figures into either "good" or "bad" people. According to DiAngelo, "We are taught to think about racism only as discrete acts committed by individual people, rather than as a complex, interconnected system."[4] Therefore, it is only when the dialogue shifts from "Was she a racist?" to "What were the ramifications of the long-term systemic racism within the organization?" that the real work can begin.

The second step to reveal systemic racism is to actively solicit multiple perspectives and viewpoints. A conversation addressing issues of race and racism will unfold differently based on who is in the room; accordingly, a group of White women may come to a different conclusion than either a mixed-race group or a single group of African American women.

Krysta Jones, a political consultant and program facilitator, believes it is imperative that organizations work to build relationships across racial lines. According to Jones, organizations should prioritize working and engaging with communities other than their own and actively seek out ways to form new partnerships.[5]

The final step requires a leap of faith. Beginning difficult conversations without a full understanding of where they will lead is problematic. Nevertheless, if our desired outcome is to reveal systemic racism, we must do more than offer a handful of new participants a seat at the table and ask them to join a conversation that is already underway. Instead, we must adjust our expectations and allow those present in the room to lead, explore, and engage in an authentic and unscripted dialogue. Janedra Sykes, who specializes in racial equity and strengthening the capacity of nonprofit organizations, offers the following guidance: "As practitioners, we need to make a commitment to being uncomfortable. In order to avoid racing to judgment on any specific group, having that group in the room and valuing their contributions is the best deterrent."[6]

For practitioners who are ready to undertake a project such as this, we need to anticipate that there will be setbacks and mistakes made in the process. However, instead of allowing these challenges to halt the work, we must take a step back and reassess, make applicable course corrections, and continue to move forward. Lori Osborne of the FWHM has framed her organization's work as a process of discovery: "This project has been a work of exploration in so many ways. We've discovered things about this time period . . . and race relations in our community, among many others things. Most importantly, we've discovered a lot about ourselves."[7] Perhaps the lesson to be learned from our peers is that this work, while not for the faint of heart, is vital to undertake. Historic sites and museums can then acknowledge the unaddressed systemic racism and begin to repair the damage.

Notes

1. Alyssa Constad, email correspondence with author, January 2019. General Federation of Women's Clubs, accessed January 18, 2019, www.gfwc.org.
2. Lori Osborne, phone interview with author, November 29, 2018.
3. Robin DiAngelo, *White Fragility: Why It's So Hard for White People to Talk about Racism* (Boston: Beacon Press, 2018), 3.
4. DiAngelo, *White Fragility*.
5. Krysta Jones, email correspondence with author, January–March 2019.
6. Janedra Sykes, email correspondence with author, May–July 2019.
7. Lori Osborne, phone interview with author, November 29, 2018.

CHAPTER 5

A United Womanhood

The General Federation of Women's Clubs and the Pursuit of Suffrage

Alyssa Constad

AT THE ELEVENTH BIENNIAL CONVENTION of the GFWC, Mrs. Charles Edson of California rose to suggest passing a resolution in support of women's suffrage. Despite the motion having been greeted with applause and approval, it was ruled "out of order" and dismissed. The biennial, held in San Francisco in June of 1912, came sixty-four years after Seneca Falls and only twenty-two years after the formation of the federation. Initially founded as a collective of literary and professional women's clubs in 1890, GFWC quickly adopted the civic causes of the progressive movement blossoming around them. The federation, primarily composed of wealthy, socially elite, White women, moved to promote public education, child labor laws, environmental regulation, and other issues that fit into the package of "domestic feminism."[1] Despite the introduction of woman's suffrage into mainstream thought more than half a century before, GFWC, as a whole, was hesitant to embrace it.

Suffrage and Clubwomen

By 1912, the question of suffrage was not new to the federation. Its ranks claimed such esteemed suffragists as Carrie Chapman Catt and Jane Addams as well as former GFWC presidents and suffragists Ellen Henrotin and Sarah Decker Platt. Clubwomen around the country shared membership with organizations such as the National Women's Suffrage

Association. State chapters, including the New York State Federation of Women's Clubs, endorsed suffrage before the national organization. However, GFWC's national leadership was hesitant to throw the federation's support behind the suffrage movement. In response to Mrs. Edson's motion, President Eva Perry Moore clarified that the resolution was "out of order" for not being "germane" to the organization and carefully stated GFWC's official position:

> I am very glad to have the opportunity of stating that it is not only the question of its [suffrage] being "germane" to the work of the organization. . . . The greater question is that whatever the majority of this convention may be, strong as it may be for citizenship—and we are all working toward citizenship—you forget that there is a minority here and at home which we wish to hold in all educational interest. . . . Do you forget that in 1900 the race issue came before the Convention as a principle from Massachusetts, from Illinois, from Colorado? There was a strong majority, but the minority in the South was recognized and we preferred to keep them with us. We wanted to work with the South, and now we want to work together as a united womanhood.[2]

To Moore, a "united womanhood" entailed a united *White* womanhood. To the federation, which was still in its youth, the ability to remain whole and unfractured through achieving the widest possible appeal to the White middle and upper classes was vital to its survival and its credibility. While GFWC did endorse suffrage only two years later at the Twelfth Biennial Convention in Chicago, their slow assent to approval was predicated on the racial- and class-based structure of the national organization.

In 1894 Josephine St. Pierre Ruffin, a Black journalist and influential suffragist, organized the New Era Club of Boston—a club comprised solely of Black women. From their founding, the New Era Club worked closely with the Massachusetts Federation of Women's Clubs and was granted membership into the state federation. In 1900, Ruffin applied to GFWC for national membership for her club and was approved by President Rebecca Douglas Lowe. That June, Ruffin arrived in Milwaukee at the Fifth Biennial Convention as the representative delegate of her club. However, she found that she was refused a seat with the other delegates. Upon learning that the New Era Club was "of the Negro race," Lowe deferred to GFWC's board of directors and the Executive Committee as to whether or not Ruffin should still be seated. Ultimately, the board of directors voted to table the issue until the next biennial meeting, and Ruffin was offered a seat as a guest of the Massachusetts Federation but not as an official delegate.[3] Ruffin declined and promptly departed.

At the same meeting, Mary Church Terrell, another major figure in the Black women's club movement, was denied permission to extend greetings to convention attendees on behalf of the National Association of Colored Women, despite having given talks to various federated clubs around the country. The "color question," and divergent ideas of how to properly resolve it, sparked widespread disagreement. Over the course of the next two years, GFWC publicly grappled with the issue and invited debate from those who wished to admit Ruffin and those who opposed the action and its implications. The debate, and its eventual resolution, had effects that would shape how GFWC would handle their political involvement and positions up through their endorsement of suffrage.

MRS. REBECCA D. LOWE.

President General Federation of Women's Clubs.

Compliments of THE CLUB WOMAN.

June, 1899.

Figure 5.1.   GFWC President Rebecca Douglas Lowe of Georgia refused clubwoman Josephine St. Pierre Ruffin a seat at GFWC's 5th Biennial Convention in 1900. Women's History and Resource Center, General Federation of Women's Clubs

The Color Question

GFWC's monthly magazine, the *Club Woman*, became the public vehicle for the issue's debate and brought regional disagreements to the forefront. In March of 1901, the *Club Woman* began printing an "Open Arena," which allowed members to state their positions on the so-called color question. In the introductory column, the editor wrote that it "had been our hope that this topic, after the Milwaukee affair, would be allowed to drop. . . . We had hoped to be able to shut all discussion of it out of our columns, but this is impossible. And so the Open Arena offers a chance to kindle intelligent discussion."[4] Despite their best efforts to disregard the situation, debate over racial integration primarily settled around geographic lines, with the Georgia Federation strenuously objecting to the admittance of Black women, and the Massachusetts Federation leading the charge to open up their membership. The Medford Women's Club of Massachusetts went so far as to withdraw from the federation in protest over the rejection of Ruffin.

Most clubs' reactions were not as severe as the Medford Women's Club, but southern states did threaten to leave the federation in the event that they were forced to integrate. Annie Johnson, president of the Georgia Federation, wrote that Georgia's warnings to leave GFWC were not "idle" and asserted that the organization should heed the southerner's advice because they understood the "the negro and his particular needs" better than their northern sisters. Johnson remarked that

> as a Northerner of many years residence in the South I want emphatically to remark that while "social equality" is now and always will be impossible at the South, yet history does not record a parallel example where a superior race with extremely limited means has done more for the moral, religious and educational training of an inferior race than have the people of the South for the negro, and that is the pain of it all to one standing on the peak knowing and loving those of both sections, that this misunderstanding should ever have arisen.[5]

In a special meeting held two months prior to the Sixth Biennial Convention in 1902, GFWC leadership decided to reach a compromise between the states. Settling on a "states' rights" position, GFWC moved not to bar Black women from becoming members of the general federation. Rather, the decision to admit women of color was left to the state federations to decide within their own membership rules. The reasoning behind the compromise was pithily summed up in a 1901 issue of the *Club Woman*:

> In a popular organization the majority must be considered. If in the future the Negro race as a whole proves to have a sufficient community of interest, if it can help us as well as get help from us, if its admission will favorably influence a large proportion of its people, let the matter then be considered frankly and fully; but in the meantime, when Southern [white] women are more than occupied with the new problems affecting them, and when it is certain that thousands of them will be antagonized and alienated by having forced upon them racial problems which they are unable to meet from the nature of things, it

seems the duty of the General Federation to consider the greatest good of the greatest number, and to preserve that sense of proportion which is the chief safeguard of a democracy and an essential quality of justice.[6]

Despite Johnson's stated belief that Black women were unable to help themselves or their communities, individual clubs around the country had already been integrating and participating in social and educational projects with Black women and Black women's clubs. After a two-year battle for admittance, the Chicago Women's Club, one of the country's largest and most influential clubs, admitted Fannie Barrier Williams, a prominent Black reformer and close friend of former president Ellen Henrotin. Various women's clubs across the country had also formed Women's Committees of the Commission on Interracial Cooperation, engaging in community projects that required racial collaboration.[7] Despite the pockets of acceptance across the federation, historian Wanda Hendricks has observed that the southern contingency triumphed because "even northern members who were uncomfortable about discriminating against elite Black women shared the beliefs of southerners about social equality."[8]

GFWC's handling of the "color question" helped to lay the groundwork for how national leadership would approach other politically polarizing issues, such as suffrage. When President Moore recalled the "race issue" in her 1912 rebuttal of the suffrage motion, she not only invoked the memory of the fissure it threatened to cause but also spoke to women's fears of *who* would be enfranchised with the passing of the Nineteenth Amendment. Mrs. Philip C. P. Barnes, a clubwoman from Kentucky, remarked that "the colored population in the South, which in some of the States exceeds the white voting population, has given us trouble that you people of the North cannot even guess. If to this we add the illiterate vote of the colored women of the South, what is to become of the white race in the South?"[9]

The Southern Contingency

Out of fear of again alienating their southern contingency, GFWC tabled the question of officially endorsing suffrage. Glenda Elizabeth Gilmore, in her study on gender and Jim Crow in North Carolina, has argued that those women who both endorsed suffrage and benefited from systems of White supremacy sought to downplay the significance of Black women voters, often trying to erase them from the equation. Rosalyn Terborg-Penn's work reinforces Gilmore's argument, noting that clubwomen viewed Black women as "invisible or expendable," and considered it "expedient to ignore their Black sisters."[10]

As suggested by Terborg-Penn, GFWC's hesitancy to officially support suffrage also stemmed from its members' socioeconomic standing and their understanding of their own roles within elite society. In her study on the relationship between clubwomen and suffragists, Karen Blair has demonstrated that GFWC produced an "uneven degree of feminism," which hindered its political progression regarding issues surrounding racism and suffrage.[11] Initially comprised of literary groups, early GFWC clubs focused on self-improvement and cultural education. As their membership expanded, women began to take an interest in civic projects and community betterment.

Municipal Housekeeping

Participation in a club, which required stepping outside the home to work within their community, deviated from nineteenth-century feminine ideals. Nonetheless, clubwomen were able to justify their choices by widening the scope of what "women's work" entailed. Blair has suggested that "to do this, they invoked the idea of Municipal Housekeeping by insisting that 'women's function, like charity, begins at home and then, like charity, goes everywhere.'"[12] Initially, suffrage had not been the aim of clubwomen, as political participation was irreconcilable with the clubwomen's goal of introducing reform through the "invocation of women's traditional domestic qualities."[13]

By 1914, however, when the resolution to endorse suffrage was again raised, many of the clubwomen had altered their understanding of political participation to fit with what they viewed as their moral duties as wives, mothers, and caretakers. The right to vote would enable women to influence school boards as well as decisions about where and when their children could work. In essence, the right to vote as a means of regulating the household was now understood as an extension of women's club work.

With the First World War looming, voting also became an urgent matter of patriotic duty. In her address to clubwomen during the 1914 Biennial in Chicago, Carrie Chapman Catt professed the moral and patriotic duty of women and the vote with dramatic flair:

> If we are ever to come to an end in this country, it will not be through any war with Mexico, nor any possible war with Japan, our danger lies within. The patriot is he who tried to find the enemy, who tried to conquer him before he has gained control over our hand, so it is not a question of right for the women of our land to have the vote, it is a question of duty, it is a question of patriotism, it is a question of women attending to the duties of their motherhood. We are mothers of the race and it is our duty to take care of that race. My sisters, over the seas there are millions of women with outstretched hands to you asking for assistance. Your own country is calling you. I know there are still women among us so medieval in spirit that they could still give their own sons and believe they are doing their highest patriotic duty . . . but I say, it is a greater duty, a greater service to this country for you to go to the polls and to put your little vote within the ballot box when it stands for the abolition of child labor.[14]

On the morning of June 13, 1914, GFWC passed a resolution endorsing "political equality of men and women" and the right of women to vote, which was only greeted by twelve "nays" and abundant cheering.[15]

While clubwomen focused much of their attention on wartime efforts and recovery over the next six years, they kept their finger on the pulse of the suffrage debate. The *Club Woman* regularly featured a "Women's Suffrage Map," updating women on the latest local developments and victories. The magazine also regularly published interviews and articles from prominent suffragists such as Dr. Anna Howard Shaw. Clubwomen such as Lizzie Crozier French, founder of the Ossoli Circle Woman's Club in Tennessee, also took on invaluable roles in securing the passage of the Nineteenth Amendment.

Figure 5.2.   GFWC Biennial Convention, May 1916. Women's History and Resource Center, General Federation of Women's Clubs

A Nuanced Legacy

Like many women's groups of the era, the GFWC leaves a complicated and nuanced legacy. As Karen Blair suggests, it is unfair "to chastise [clubwomen] for reluctant feminism"; to do so is to ignore the fact that clubwomen developed their own methods of combating women's limited place within the home.[16] However, it is also essential that in recounting the story of the path to suffrage, we acknowledge that the positions and privileges of clubwomen—and other women within their elite sphere—were built on the shoulders of those who they left behind, and often disenfranchised. Clubwomen across the country worked with Black women and Black women's clubs at the turn of the century with the common goal of community betterment. However, as the goal of the Nineteenth Amendment became more tangible, interracial cooperation was abandoned from fear of limiting the appeal of the organization and losing the battle for the vote.

Today, the GFWC continues to advocate for the rights and the advancement of women. Housed in a National Historic Landmark, GFWC Headquarters is located within a building that clubwomen purchased only two years after the passage of the Nineteenth Amendment. GFWC is also home to the WHRC, which collects, preserves, and interprets the history of GFWC. The WHRC is open to the public, and their records have helped numerous scholars piece together the story of American suffrage and myriad other landmark achievements in the history of the United States. Their archives still have much more to contribute to the field of women's history.

GFWC's archives should play a key role in shaping and reassessing the organization's narrative around suffrage. As an organization that still has an active membership, dedicated conversation and action are also necessary in moving forward and understanding its legacy and its consequential implications. GFWC's national leadership has taken the initial step to encourage conversation, reflection, and action around the organization's history. The writing of this article presented the Executive Committee with an outlet for discussion and education. Yet, while this piece presented a tangible step in considering history and legacy, it also remains the only step taken, and the conversation has not continued with the greater membership of GFWC.

GFWC's history of exclusion continues to be visible in their membership. Although the organization is not as financially exclusive as it was one hundred years ago, it is still primarily comprised of middle- and upper-middle-class White women. There are currently no women of color who hold leadership positions at the national level, nor have there been since the 1930s.[17]

At an 1889 meeting of women's club delegates, one year before the clubs would federate, Ella Dietz Clymer remarked to the group that "we look for unity, but unity in diversity; we hope that you will enrich us by your varied experience, and let us pledge ourselves to work for a common cause, the cause of united womanhood throughout the world."[18] As GFWC continues to ignore its past, its unity comes at the price of its diversity.

Notes

1. Karen Blair, *The Clubwoman as Feminist: True Womanhood Redefined, 1868–1914* (New York: Holmes and Meier, 1980), 4–5. In *The Clubwoman as Feminist*, historian Karen Blair borrows the term *domestic feminism* from Daniel Scott Smith to expand its definition in application to literary clubs and clubwomen of the late nineteenth and early twentieth centuries. Blair claims that in "the politicization of Domestic Feminism . . . woman nurtured pride in the lady's special qualities and confidence to reach out into the public domain."

2. Phebe M. Welch, ed., *The General Federation of Women's Clubs: Eleventh Biennial Convention: Official Report* (Newark: The Federation, 1912), 603.

3. Emma A. Fox, ed., *General Federation of Women's Clubs: Sixth Biennial Convention: Official Proceedings* (Detroit: John Bornman and Son, 1902), 25.

4. "The Open Arena," *Club Woman*, March 1901, 180.

5. Annie E. Johnson, "A Word from Georgia," *Club Woman*, March 1901, 183.

6. Elizabeth King Elliot, "The Race Problems in the General Federation," *Club Woman*, October 1901, 12.

7. Glenda Elizabeth Gilmore, *Gender & Jim Crow: Women and the Politics of White Supremacy in North Carolina 1896–1920* (Chapel Hill: University of North Carolina Press, 1996), 201.

8. Wanda A. Hendricks, *Fannie Barrier Williams: Crossing the Borders of Region and Race* (Urbana: University of Illinois Press, 2014), 124.

9. As quoted in Blair, *Clubwoman as Feminist*, 112.

10. Rosalyn Terborg-Penn, *African American Women in the Struggle for the Vote, 1850–1920* (Bloomington: Indiana University Press, 1998), 134.
11. Blair, *Clubwoman as Feminist*, 108.
12. Blair, *Clubwoman as Feminist*, 106.
13. Blair, *Clubwoman as Feminist*, 111.
14. Carrie Chapman Catt, "The World Progress of Women," *General Federation of Women's Clubs Magazine*, July 1914, 21.
15. Catt, "The World Progress of Women," 19; Alyssa Constad, *Votes For Women*, GFWC, Summer 2019, www.gfwc.org/summer-2019. Words for this post were originally borrowed from a first draft of this chapter.
16. Blair, *Clubwoman as Feminist*, 114.
17. In 1935 Roberta Campbell Lawson, a member of the Delaware Tribe, was elected international president.
18. Mary Jean Houde, *Reaching Out: A Story of the General Federation of Women's Clubs* (Chicago: Mobium Press, 1989), 27.

CHAPTER 6

The National Woman's Party

Jennifer Krafchik[1]

IN HER OPENING REMARKS AT THE "A Woman's Perspective: Women in American Democracy" symposium held at the SBHM, the home of the historic NWP, on October 4, 2011, Ambassador Carol Moseley Braun said, "It is up to us to make the history of the civil and women's rights and human rights struggles a living thing, so that the conclusions the younger generation reaches about 'why' will be grounded in the whole truth."[2] During this event, the NWP unveiled new exhibits and programs for the first time in more than ten years, which were meant to expand the public's understanding of the history of the women's voting movement and larger twentieth-century women's rights movement.

The NWP was a key organization during the final seven-year push for the Nineteenth Amendment, and later with the introduction of the ERA. Always small and slightly polarizing, history has also revealed that the NWP was an organization deeply flawed in leadership, its narrow mission statement, and its focus on a small group of "heroic" women rather than the NWP's significance to the larger women's rights movement. The challenge for the Belmont-Paul Women's Equality National Monument going forward is how to interpret the NWP's tactics and strategies in ways that acknowledge these flaws and still have a substantial impact on historical analysis of the women's rights movement and its ongoing significance for women today. As public historians and interpreters, will this knowledge allow us to answer interpretive questions, such as, "Who is missing from this room and why?"

Beginning in 1929, the NWP operated its fifth headquarters at 144 Constitution Avenue NE on Capitol Hill in Washington, DC. The site became a staging ground for the NWP's advocacy for women's political, social, and economic equality. Designated as a National Historic Landmark in 1974, it was the only site in the United States dedicated to the twentieth-century women's movement.

The NWP operated as a lobbying organization until 1997, when it became a 501(c)3 educational nonprofit known as the SBHM. In 2016 President Barack Obama designated the museum as the Belmont-Paul Women's Equality National Monument and now NPS owns and operates the museum, while the NWP retains ownership and stewardship of its archival collection. Today, the NWP educates the public about the women's rights movement and collaborates with NPS to provide a forum for dialogue and community conversation. The goal is to engage new generations to find their civic voices and become part of social, economic, and political change throughout the world.

The Sewall-Belmont House

Upon entering the main hallway, first-time visitors to SBHM in 2001 might have recognized several details: first, the heroic busts—Susan B. Anthony, Lucretia Mott, and Elizabeth Cady Stanton, or simply the "big three." In one gallery, there was a modern sculpture of Sojourner Truth.[3] Along the staircase were reproduced black and white images of other African American women, such as Mary Ann Shadd Cary, Josephine St. Pierre Ruffin, Althea Gibson, Fannie Lou Hamer, Dorothy Height, and at least ten other women who most visitors probably did not recognize. This was the only label:

> African-American Suffragists: These women were among the many Black women who campaigned for suffrage. They were also involved with many other political issues pertinent to their race including anti-lynching campaigns, segregation, and access to and equality in education.[4]

In 2001, historic houses routinely included "no touching" signs and velvet ropes, and SBHM was no different. Docents told the story through furniture vignettes rather than artifacts and archival materials. The guided tours often made reference to legends and partially unsubstantiated stories, rather than the factual and undoubtedly complicated story of the women of the NWP. To address much-needed changes, SBHM would soon embark on an interpretive planning project, which was largely staff led, with some involvement from select board members who had a specific interest in assisting with that process.

Historical Overview

Originally under the auspices of the National American Woman Suffrage Association (NAWSA), the Congressional Union split from the NAWSA in 1914 due to differences in strategy. Alice Paul formed the independent NWP in 1916 with a philosophy of holding the party in power responsible. The NWP would withhold its support from the existing political parties until women had gained the right to vote. Under Paul's leadership, the NWP worked for a federal suffrage amendment that targeted elected officials through a revolutionary strategy of sustained dramatic and nonviolent protest.

Many NWP leaders learned about the suffrage movement while in England working with the Pankhurst family. Activists engaged in visible measures such as heckling, window-smashing, and rock-throwing to raise public awareness of the fight for the right to vote.

Alice Paul, Lucy Burns, Inez Milholland, and others joined the British suffragette movement and participated in demonstrations. They were arrested and imprisoned. In jail, they participated in hunger strikes to protest their confinement and were force-fed. When Paul, Burns, and others returned to the United States in 1910, they were determined to bring these tactics back with them.

The women of the NWP were on the cutting edge of nonviolent activism: they utilized pageantry, propaganda, and passive resistance to exert public pressure on both political parties. They were the first to picket the White House, beginning in January 1917, a daring move that continued until Congress passed the Nineteenth Amendment in 1919. When the United States entered WWI, the pickets highlighted the hypocrisy in supporting democracy abroad while denying women's rights at home. Their punishment included violent arrests and imprisonment. Protesting the horrific conditions in jail and demanding they be treated as political prisoners, suffragists also went on hunger strikes and were force-fed.

Figure 6.1.   New York State Day on the picket line at the White House, January 26, 1917. National Woman's Party, Washington, DC

Although the NWP were progressive for the time, they condoned racist actions that marginalized Black women in the movement. For example, during the March 1913 parade, Black suffragists were segregated at the back of the procession instead of being permitted to march with their respective state delegations. Alpha Suffrage Club president Ida B. Wells-Barnett rejected the instructions and marched instead with the White Chicago delegation. Racial divisions between the major suffrage organizations including the NWP and African American women would continue to grow.

From 1914 to 1915, the NWP's *The Suffragist* published editorials making the case that White women should not be afraid of African American women voters because White women would outnumber them. The editorials were intended to increase support in the southern states for a federal amendment. NWP members also made public statements such as "the enfranchising of all women will increase the relative power of the white race in a most remarkable way" and "the enfranchisement of Southern women would enormously increase the white supremacy."[5]

On August 26, 1920, the country celebrated the passage of the Nineteenth Amendment. NAWSA rebranded as the League of Women Voters and focused on getting women out to vote. The oldest African American women's club, the National Association of Colored Women—while battling countless injustices during the Jim Crow era—continued an unrelenting pursuit of full, unfettered citizenship for all people. And the NWP began campaigning for complete constitutional equality for women.

The Nineteenth Amendment enshrined women's vote in the Constitution but did not protect any other rights for women. To fill this gap, Alice Paul and other NWP members drafted the original version of the ERA in 1923 as a natural completion of the suffrage amendment.

The decision to focus almost exclusively on the ERA had long-lasting consequences for the NWP.[6] Though the Nineteenth Amendment was a legislative victory, it did not guarantee all women the right to exercise their vote freely. States put obstacles, including long wait times, poll taxes, and literacy testing in place to prevent women of color from voting. African American voters also experienced ongoing violence. Alice Paul and the NWP chose not to support the fight for fair access to the ballot for all women. In doing so, they further alienated many women of color who had worked for suffrage and might have previously supported the NWP.

A Nebulous Interpretation Plan

In 2001, the NWP was still in transition from a lobbying organization into a nonprofit with a full-time staff. Part-time docents led board-approved tours, but they added their own research to augment the story. This research focused on topics ranging from in-depth examinations of the fine arts on display to additional facts about the uses of the historic headquarters, NWP history, and membership. The museum consisted mostly of rooms filled with desks, chairs, large bedsteads and armoires, decrepit bookcases, and portraits of NWP members.

As one of the first four institutions to receive a grant from the federal Save America's Treasures program, SBHM completed a Historic Structures Report and began work on an eight-phase restoration plan slated to take six to eight years to complete. The house closed for nearly a year from 2001 to 2002 in an effort to complete a $1.5 million restoration that included critical exterior and structural improvements. Ultimately only the first two phases were completed, as the funding for the projects ran out by 2009.

Unfortunately, when the house reopened, outdated interpretative methods continued. Visitors still could not view the rich collections buried in storage, including the banners carried in front of the White House, the iconic photographs, and the congressional lobbying cards. African American women's contributions were referenced in the house, but mentioned only in passing, and did not address the racial divide.

In an attempt to portray the NWP as an inclusive organization, docents made broad statements, indicating that the NWP was one of the few organizations that permitted African American women to join, mentioning women such as Mary Church Terrell as members and also suggesting that Mahatma Gandhi and Martin Luther King Jr. were inspired by the NWP strategy of nonviolent protest. Although "technically" accurate, these statements lacked a nuanced understanding of the pervasive racism condoned by the NWP and experienced by women of color within the suffrage movement.

As the SBHM staff began to grow and evolve, attempts to flesh out the interpretation, learn more about the historical details, and create inclusive programs began to take shape. In 2002, the NWP engaged a professional museum consultant to undertake a new interpretation plan. For the first time, staff began to view period rooms more like exhibition galleries.

Telling Half of the Story

Nonetheless, the final plan was flawed in that it included no discussion of the lack of resources specific to interpretation of women of color within the NWP collection. Suggesting that the exhibits include women of color, but not addressing the lack of archival resources as a barrier to doing so, made it a difficult process, at best. The NWP also struggled with lackluster funding, too few staff, and not enough time for planning. In addition, the sporadic nature of funding did not allow staff or board members enough time to plan and carry out projects with more thoughtful reflection of both the NWP's history and the collection. Consequently, the staff did not conduct a thorough collections evaluation. In spite of these factors, the writing began and the interpretive plan was completed in 2003.

In 2003, the NWP then received a grant from the DC Humanities Council to publish a booklet featuring twenty-three Black women activists titled *Black Women in America: Contributors to Our Heritage*. In the introduction, historian Elsa Barkley Brown states, "In highlighting these women's accomplishments, the Sewall-Belmont House and Museum recognizes the range of strategies women have employed in their political struggles and presents us with an understanding of the broad range of women's history of politics."[7] The booklet served as a guide to the exhibit of the same name on display in SBHM, and staff distributed the popular booklets to museum visitors, schools, and educational groups.

Figure 6.2.   Cover of "Black Women in America: Contributors to our Heritage" published by the NWP in 2003. National Woman's Party, Washington, DC

This publication was followed by a new bus tour titled "Journey toward Equality," a collaboration between the NWP and the Frederick Douglass National Historic Site in the Anacostia neighborhood of Washington, DC, and the Mary McLeod Bethune Council House National Historic Site in Washington, DC. Sponsored by NPS, the popular tour was led by the NWP's docent and interpretation coordinator, Jessica Tava, and ran for more than two years. However, when NPS was unable to continue to fund the tour, the program ended and efforts toward inclusive interpretation ceased.

New Funding Highlights Old Problems

In 2010, SBHM was the recipient of two congressionally directed grants through the Department of the Interior, NPS, and the Institute for Museum and Library Services (IMLS) in the amount of $2 million (the original request outlined a need for $8 million). Due to the restrictive nature of the funding, staff had less than eleven months from receipt of the grants to fully expend the funds, which allowed for almost no advance planning for interpretation, construction, or the financial implications of fully closing the museum for almost a year. NPS funding was strictly for construction projects, such as a new fire sprinkler system in the main house; 80 percent ADA accessibility; and critical repairs to exterior elements of the site including the staircases and fire escapes. The IMLS funding was designated to reinterpret permanent exhibits on the first floor as well as catalog, preserve, and provide public access to the NWP collection. When completed, staff and consultants had cataloged and re-housed over ten thousand objects, conserved twenty-two individual items, wrote an environmental improvement plan, installed new permanent exhibitions, created a new website and mobile application, and produced a day-long symposium titled "A Woman's Perspective: Women in American Democracy."

As part of the project, in 2010 the NWP staff updated the original 2003 interpretive plan. They also formed an advisory committee to examine and analyze the NWP collection, resulting in individual internal reports from several scholars that were used internally by NWP staff to determine the strongest areas for research. The committee included Dr. Kyle Ciani, associate professor of history at Illinois State University; Dr. Ellen Carol DuBois, professor of history at UCLA; and Dr. Allida Black, research professor of history and international affairs at the George Washington University. In her report, DuBois writes: "While there are other archives and museums devoted to the history of American women, none is so clearly focused on the history of feminism as is Sewall Belmont."[8] Ciani, in particular, shares a useful analysis of the existing historiography that would drive later interpretive decisions:

> The SBHM remains wedded to what has been termed the "compensatory" and "contributory" means of communicating women's history, which highlights and lauds the societal accomplishments made by women. One need only walk into the main entry to experience the stunted development of SBHM interpretation by its use of monumental, "great figures" artifacts, such as the hallway sculptures and Alice Paul's bedroom furniture. While the sculptures are eye-catching (and, admittedly, fun to have one's photo taken next to) they do not help to communicate the diversity and complexity of the woman's movement.[9]

Ciani's report drove the larger discussion, which articulated the need to include a more nuanced interpretation of the artifacts in future exhibits. If the staff had followed her advice, Ciani's framework would have resulted in a deeper examination of the relationships between various groups during the suffrage and equal rights movements, dug deeper into the contributions and decisions made by those "monumental, 'great figures,'" and provided visitors with a more nuanced and inclusive story of the twentieth-century women's rights movement.

Staff also created an Interpretation Advisory Committee (IAC) to facilitate the interpretive and exhibits planning process and to strengthen partnerships with similar organizations.[10] Recognizing that the hidden collections would be critical to the success of any interpretation moving forward, the IAC advised the staff on interpretation planning including tour formats, the role and use of artifacts and technology, utilization of the website and other social media to supplement physical exhibits, and visitor flow. The contents of the meetings were compiled into a comprehensive report used to create an interpretive plan for the exhibition designer, which included this guiding statement:

> The principal story of the Sewall-Belmont House and Museum is the relevance, evolution, and context of the National Woman's Party. The story includes topics such as woman's suffrage, tactics and strategies, domestic efforts to battle discriminatory laws, the fight for the Equal Rights Amendment, racism and discrimination within the NWP, and the international campaigns for women's equality.[11]

Unfortunately, even with this clear directive, the house reopened in May 2011 with few images of women of color and an almost complete exclusion of the significance of race during the suffrage and equal rights movements. In one gallery, a portrait of Frederick Douglass (on display in the house since 2001) was reinstalled, but the story of Ida B. Wells's decision to enter the March 3, 1913, parade with her chosen delegation was excluded. The Hall of Portraits, which included images and photographs of NWP members, and intro-

Figure 6.3.   Origins Gallery of the Belmont-Paul Women's Equality National Monument, 2016. National Woman's Party, Washington, DC

duced discussions about the "community of women" and the women's equality movement, included no women of color. This was despite the fact that Mary Church Terrell was a known NWP member and her story would have allowed for discussions about her challenges with trying to communicate with Alice Paul and the NWP.

Where was the breakdown that prevented the implementation of the plan? It came down to timing and funding. Due to restrictions on the grant money, the staff was forced to condense what should have been two years of interpretive planning and research into only a few weeks or lose the funding. This type of funding, while seemingly a miraculous windfall to a small organization, often has long-term negative implications. When forced to make hasty decisions about historical interpretation, sometimes stories are crafted according to the surface that practitioners see in front of them instead of the layers that live behind. Thus, the results are inherently flawed.

Unfortunately, the grant process also did not provide sufficient time for the board and staff to secure the additional funding needed to keep SBHM afloat during the ten-month museum closure. To finance the closure, the board relied on a line of credit to cover operations so the staff leadership and NWP board had to focus almost exclusively on fundraising.

In addition to significant time constraints, the staff writing the exhibit text and object list had little knowledge and expertise on the role of women of color during the suffrage movement. Additionally, an assessment of the collection confirmed that there was little available to pull from, and there was so little time to finalize the exhibit text that no one had the opportunity to research outside of the NWP collection. Rather than do an incomplete or inaccurate job, staff chose to omit the content and fully address it after the renovation project. When SBHM reopened in May 2011, the staff attempted to identify the existing flaws in interpretation and how to resolve them. With more visitors to the site, however, the absence of diversity became more apparent and urgent to correct.

After the Belmont-Paul Women's Equality National Monument was established in 2016, NPS and the NWP formalized the public-private partnership through a governing general agreement, followed by a foundation document that provides guidance for planning and management of the site. Because the house was renamed the "women's equality monument," both NPS and the NWP agreed that there is a much broader mandate for discussions of women's equality beyond the narrow history of the NWP.

In 2018, NPS and NWP completed a joint long-range interpretive plan, which includes the following statement: "New partnerships and programs must be able to reach people across the country and the world, particularly at times when the house itself is closed. They should also seek to improve people's understanding of how women of all races and backgrounds shaped the country and continue to work toward equality today."[12] The goals for a revised interpretation and strategy will include sharing a larger story that appeals to a wider audience and creates a call to action.

What the Future Holds

There is still much work to be done. In 2019, the NWP opened a new traveling exhibition, "Standing Together: Women's Fight for Full Equality," at the University of Richmond

Downtown Center for Civic Engagement. This five-panel exhibition discusses the suffrage and equal rights movements, focuses on the diverse organizations and groups of women and their experiences, and more directly addresses the racism and complicated outcomes of the movement then and now. The Belmont-Paul closed for renovation in 2020. During the closure, the goal is to revisit all of the exhibits and interpretation, and upon reopening in 2023 the exhibits and artifacts on display will share a much broader, more candid history, with less focus on individual "heroes" and more focus on dialogue and action.

The story of the NWP is challenging to share and to discuss with the public. Over time, historical understanding of the NWP's complicated history and the future of the organization continue to evolve. Our ability to gauge and assess revered icons continues to be increasingly convoluted as we read more diverse scholarship and discover the hidden facts within the NWP collection. The lack of artifacts, documents, and other historical information about women of color tells a very critical story in and of itself, one that should be incorporated into Belmont-Paul's interpretation of Alice Paul's leadership, as well as the decisions made by all women's organizations, and the choice to fight for the ERA instead of voting rights for women of color. Interpretation of those facts would lead to critical and necessary evaluation of the success and failures of the suffrage movement and its implications for women today and into the future.

Notes

1. Originally hired as a temporary research intern, I joined the staff as a part-time collections assistant to process the photograph collection in 2001. From there, I was hired as the full-time education and collections coordinator to develop new educational and interpretive programs and continue work on collections processing. As the staff evolved, I became the full-time collections manager.

2. Carol Moseley Braun, "Keynote Remarks" (lecture), A Woman's Perspective: Women in American Democracy Symposium, Sewall-Belmont House and Museum, Washington, DC, October 4, 2011.

3. Inge Hardison, *Sojourner Truth*, Bronze, Sewall-Belmont House & Museum, Washington, DC, 1968. This bronze sculpture was a gift of the Negro Business and Professional Women's Clubs Inc. of New York, given in 1995.

4. Label, Stairwell, *Black Women in America: Contributors to Our Heritage* (exhibit), Sewall-Belmont House and Museum, Washington, DC, 2001.

5. "National Suffrage and the Race Problem," *The Suffragist* 2, no. 46 (1914): 8; Helena Hill Weed, "The Federal Amendment and the Race Problem," *The Suffragist* 3, no. 6 (1915): 3.

6. The current version of the ERA reads: "Equality of rights under the law shall not be denied or abridged by the United States on account of sex." The ERA has been introduced in almost every session of Congress since it passed in 1972 and went to the states for ratification. However, Congress added a ten-year deadline for the process, and the ERA fell three states short of the required thirty-eight states to become law. Today, efforts continue toward its passage, but the NWP has long since ceased lobbying efforts and ceded its place in the ERA Movement.

7. National Woman's Party, *Black Women in America: Contributors to Our Heritage* (Washington, DC: Sewall-Belmont House and Museum, 2003).

8. Ellen Carol DuBois, "Sewall-Belmont House & Museum Collection Assessment," 2010.

9. Kyle E. Ciani, "Sewall-Belmont House & Museum Collection Assessment," 2010.

10. IAC members included representatives from the Smithsonian National Museum of American History, the National Trust for Historic Preservation, the Library of Congress, several universities, and local museums as well as museum assistants, staff, and board members.

11. National Woman's Party, "Sewall-Belmont House and Museum Interpretive Plan," 2010.

12. History Associates, "Belmont-Paul Women's Equality National Monument Interpretive Plan," December 4, 2018.

CHAPTER 7

Truth-Telling

Frances Willard and Ida B. Wells, a Project of the Frances Willard House Museum

Lori Osborne[1]

Frances Willard and the Woman's Christian Temperance Union

AS PRESIDENT OF THE WCTU from 1879 to 1898, Frances Willard (1839–1898) was known for her work to prevent the negative impact of alcohol on society, especially women and children, and her lifelong mission to advance women's rights. Her development of the "Home Protection" argument in support of women's suffrage provided a critical strategy for the movement and, once she persuaded the membership of the WCTU to join her, added thousands of women to the cause. By the mid-1890s the WCTU was the largest organization of women in the United States, with a broad social reform agenda, and had grown into a worldwide and diverse organization.

Willard and her family had been abolitionists before the Civil War and she carried this legacy into her work in the WCTU. Willard encouraged Black membership in the WCTU and spoke to Black audiences. Noted Black leaders complimented her for this progressive (for the time) leadership, including Frederick Douglass, who said she was "devoted to the cause of the colored people."[2] Under Willard's leadership, the WCTU established a national Department of Work among the "colored people" headed by African American women. Black women were also involved in local WCTU groups throughout the country—sometimes integrated with White women, more often as separate chapters.

However, Willard also carried with her a middle-class White woman's limited perspective on race. Willard made public comments that were demeaning to Black people and

Figure 7.1. Frances Willard (1839–1898). Courtesy Woman's Christian Temperance Union Archives, Evanston, Illinois. Women's Christian Temperance Union Archives

other people of color, reflecting the underlying racism that permeated our nation's culture. She also believed and encouraged racist propaganda and did not speak out strongly against lynching as it became an increasing problem in the 1880s and 1890s.

Ida B. Wells

Ida B. Wells (1862–1931) was an educator and journalist who began her civil rights activism in response to racist incidents she experienced in Memphis, Tennessee. Born into slavery in Mississippi, Wells had moved to Memphis in 1883 to further her teaching career, working to support herself and her siblings after her parents died in a yellow fever epidemic.

In 1884, Wells was forcibly removed from a train car because of her race, and she subsequently sued the railroad for infringement of her rights. She wrote about the incident in a local newspaper and began writing on race issues for local and national newspapers. In 1889 she became co-owner of *Free Speech and Headlight*, a Memphis newspaper. In 1891 she was removed from her teaching position because of her outspoken views.

After three close Memphis friends were unjustly arrested and lynched by a White mob in 1892, Wells began to look further into the growing number of lynching incidents in the United States. Using her journalism connections and investigative abilities, Wells began shedding light on the larger problem and calling national leaders to account. In 1892, she published the pamphlet "Southern Horrors: Lynch Law in All Its Phases" and later that year the offices of *Free Speech and Headlight* were destroyed by a mob. Wells moved to Chicago and began a public speaking career to raise awareness and change public sentiment about lynching.

Willard and Wells

By 1895, Wells's anti-lynching campaign was well underway, but she was frustrated by the reluctance of influential White reformers such as Willard to support her work. Willard had made racially charged statements in a newspaper interview given in 1890, and Wells had seen and remembered the interview. While on a speaking tour of England in 1894, Wells republished the interview, calling into question Willard's moral leadership and using it to apply pressure on Willard to live up to her reputation as a Christian reformer.

In the interview, Willard had invoked what Wells described as "the old threadbare lie that negro men rape white women" and had used statements such as "the colored race multiplies like the locusts of Egypt" and "the grog [liquor] shop is its centre of power." Wells charged that Willard's position as an internationally known Christian reformer, and the leader of an organization with many African American women members, carried a special duty to speak out against the violence of lynching, rather than perpetuate the stereotype that drunken Black men threatened "the safety of woman, of childhood, of the home."[3]

During the early 1890s, however, Willard was making a conscious push to grow the membership of the WCTU among White women in the South. While alcohol was a serious problem in the Black community, leading to strong support of temperance by Black women, alcohol and drunkenness were also used by Whites to stereotype and discriminate against Blacks and other minority groups. White leaders in the women's temperance and suffrage movements made questionable moral compromises by using these racist stereotypes to encourage support and growth for their causes among southern White women. The most extreme and violent result of this was lynching.

Wells confronted Willard directly, calling on her and the WCTU to explicitly denounce lynching. At first, Willard tried to defend herself, insisting she had "not an atom of race prejudice," citing her family's involvement with the abolition movement and her work supporting African American women in the WCTU.[4] In the face of mounting pressure, Willard eventually took measures to address the issue, including speaking out publicly against lynching. The WCTU passed anti-lynching resolutions in 1894, 1895, and several years following. The conflict attracted international attention and even condemnation of the WCTU and Willard.

Willard died in 1898 with this conflict unresolved. Wells continued to work against racism and injustice until her death in 1931, not hesitating to criticize White women reformers when she believed they ignored or perpetuated racial discrimination.

The Goal of the Truth-Telling Project

The Frances Willard House Museum is located at Willard's family home in Evanston, Illinois. The house has been a museum since 1900 and was managed by the WCTU for most of those years. In addition, the WCTU Archives is also at the site and hold Willard's personal papers and the WCTUs organizational records. Both the museum and archives are now run by a separate nonprofit organization whose goal is to tell the full story of the woman's temperance movement as well as to promote education about women's wider social reform efforts in this time period and how they have shaped our world today.

Figure 7.2. Frances Willard House Museum, a National Historic Landmark, Evanston, Illinois. The house was constructed in 1865 by Willard's father. It was her home from 1865 until her death in 1898. The house museum opened in 1900, making it one of the earliest historic sites dedicated to a woman's life. Women's Christian Temperance Union Archives

As part of this work, the FWHM staff and board made a commitment to tell the truth of the conflict between Willard and Wells and to present all sides of Willard's life and work. Our primary purpose was to revisit Willard's original unmet goals and continue the work she began to advance women's rights and promote a just and equitable world for all. We aimed to honestly examine Willard's failure of leadership on this issue and invite our community (in Evanston and beyond) to explore the story for themselves. More broadly, this project hoped to address the conflict between these two significant American women as just one part of the complex and ongoing story of racism in America and American women's movements.

Digital Collection and Online Exhibit

The first phase of our work was research into what actually happened in the exchanges between Willard and Wells. With the help of a graduate student team in the Public History Department at Loyola University of Chicago, the original newspaper articles, speeches, correspondence, and other archival material were gathered and described in a draft online exhibit and collection. One of the students, Loyola PhD student Ella Wagner, was hired to complete the construction of the exhibit. The launch of *Truth-Telling: Frances Willard and Ida B. Wells—a Documentary Website* took place in March of 2019 (willardandwells.org).

The website consists of an interactive timeline, contextual information, and interpretive essays that helps readers understand the conflict and encourages them to explore what happened and draw their own conclusions. It features the primary sources (many of them held at the Willard Archives and previously unknown) that tell the story of the dispute, including newspaper articles, correspondence, speeches, and other material. Users are able to follow links from the sources to short essays on some of the relevant context: temperance, suffrage, reconstruction, and short biographies of Willard and Wells, among others. Interpretative essays by scholars, museum staff, and community members—including Wells's great-granddaughter, Michelle Duster—also reflect on the material. A bibliography and list of other relevant resources are included as well.

While we drew conclusions from these materials and the research we have done, we also made the materials available for research by the public. We hoped that by doing this foundational research work, and creating and sharing this digital collection, we could encourage a larger understanding of the ways racism permeated our culture and how that affects our world today.

Community Conversations

A big part of our plan was to hold small and large community conversations about the conflict, to tell the story, to discuss the issues it raises, and to listen and learn. To some extent, the entire project arose from community feedback, as the story of the conflict had become much more public in the last few years. We have had many informal conversations and are continuing more formal meetings, public programs, and other outreach to share the story with our community. Because we are historians, we are skilled at research and analysis, at seeing what happened and placing it in context. But we strongly feel that we must let the community tell the story back to us from different perspectives, so that we can hear it in the world today and learn its impact in a new way.

Evanston is a large and diverse suburb just north of Chicago. It has its own history of racism and struggles to tell that story and to confront the issues that linger today. In 2019 and the beginning of 2020, our conversations in Evanston were with a handful of local community leaders, including leaders in the Black community. We have also had discussions with students, faculty, and staff at Northwestern University, which is based in Evanston, including staff from Northwestern's Provost's Office, History Department, and University Archives. Willard was the first dean of women at Northwestern and many things on campus are named for her, so the issue of her legacy on this issue is a critical one for Northwestern.

We also connected to the celebration of 150 years of coeducation at the university that took place in the fall of 2019.

In addition, we expanded our discussions to Chicago, which was Wells's home for most of her adult life. Though there is not a historic site for Wells in the city (her home is privately owned), there are many organizations that share her story and are specifically working to document and memorialize her work. We believe that allowing this conflict to be reexamined through the voices of Willard and Wells, and through the organizations that represent them now, is one possible way to find the common ground they struggled to find long ago.

To some extent, the work of this project is meant to be an ongoing part of our work, as we anticipate the need for ongoing conversations and discussions. We also imagine and hope that this work will change how we work and how our organization operates. Though we do not have specific goals related to this, our overall goal is to grow more diverse in our perspectives and our leadership. We want to become a place where the exploration of the past leads us to challenge ourselves and our community—to create a greater understanding of the present and find new ways to move forward.

Public Programs

While this project has been underway, we have been engaging with the Evanston community through small programs and partnerships. In 2017, the FWHM hosted members of the Evanston Black Lives Matter group while they were working on a Witness Quilt to document the Black women whose lives had been lost to gun violence that year. We also hosted the Evanston Public Library Evanston Reads book program on *Citizen* (by Claudia Rankine) and discussed the conflict between Willard and Wells with the group. We documented Evanston's African American women's history in the Tour Evanston Women's History map. Though not directly connected to the Wells and Willard story, these efforts are ways of expanding our work and connecting to the issue of race in other ways.

Our visiting artist project in spring and summer 2018 with photographer Vanessa Filley was part of this work as well. She spent a month learning about Willard and the WCTU through conversations with museum staff and volunteers and her own reading and research. She examined original photos and archival materials in the collection. She then chose to address the issue of race (and particularly the story of the conflict between Willard and Wells) and created a series of depictions of diverse women at the house—repopulating the rooms with women whose stories and faces had been ignored or erased. The resulting photographs were powerful and disruptive, causing staff, volunteers, and visitors to examine their preconceptions of the story of Willard and the WCTU.

We have also discussed this project at several conferences. In April 2018, Ella Wagner was part of a National Council on Public History poster session. In July 2018, at the joint conference of the Illinois Association of Museums and the Association of Midwest Museums, I discussed this project as part of a session on using historic sites for civic engagement. The overall issue of racism in the women's movement was also the subject of several panel discussions that I was involved in at the AASLH conference in September.

The public phase of "Truth-Telling" began in 2019. In February we held a public program with Carole Stewart, the author of a new book on African American women in the temperance movement. In March we launched the documentary website with a public program and panel discussion. More than two hundred people attended this event. We had good questions during the event and helpful feedback afterward. Additionally, we have shared information with the Evanston League of Women Voters and participated in a panel discussion at the Evanston Equity Summit, hosted by the Evanston/North Shore YWCA.

Figure 7.3. Truth-Telling: Frances Willard and Ida B. Wells website. This screenshot of the website shows the introductory page. Courtesy Frances Willard House Museum. Frances Willard House Museum

Finally, we incorporated all of this work into planning for Evanston's and Illinois's commemoration of the ratification of the Nineteenth Amendment in 2020. A big part of anniversary discussions was to recognize that not all women achieved the right to vote when the amendment passed. Voting rights were still restricted, especially along racial lines, and thus the anniversary needed to be a recognition of the great achievement that occurred in 1920 as well as the work that still needed (and still needs) to be done for full voting rights. We had multiple discussions with leaders at other historic sites who faced similar issues, including women's history sites, and planning groups for the 2020 women's suffrage anniversary. To some extent, this was the underlying reason for us taking on the Truth-Telling Project—and was a significant achievement of the 2020 year. Telling the whole story of race and racism in the women's suffrage movement was a huge challenge—as was finding and telling the story of Black suffragists and their work for voting rights for all.

To this end, we connected with Jane Addams Hull House Museum in Chicago and once again with Northwestern University and offered a series of talks throughout 2020 that addressed racism in the women's suffrage movement. The series was titled "With You or Not at All" and took inspiration from Ida B. Wells and her response to attempted exclusion from a 1913 Washington, DC, suffrage parade. The three-part series concluded with a panel discussion that explored the connections and conflicts between Frances Willard, Ida B. Wells, and Jane Addams as three Chicago-based reformers and activists. We also worked with WTTW (our local PBS station) to tell the story of the conflict and highlight Wells's activist work in Chicago. Our fall 2020 intern worked on researching the stories of Black women in the WCTU and created a draft database and research report. We plan to continue this work in the future. These are just some of the many places where discussion of race and the issues raised in the Truth-Telling Project has taken place. It has truly been integrated into almost everything we do.

Barriers and Issues Faced

As a small historic site with a very limited budget, prioritizing this work has been hard to do. There are many things demanding resources of time and money, and focusing on this project has been a challenge. Thankfully, we had the Loyola student project that really allowed us to get started. We could then see what needed to be done and begin to plan for the larger project. We understood how much time needed to be spent on background research and assembling the primary sources. We could also see how the website would need to be complemented by public outreach and programs.

Though we applied for grants to fund the final website production and community programs, we did not receive funding. The responses to our grants were generally that we were not set up to do such a project, that we did not have a large enough base of support to draw on, and that our board was not diverse. We felt, alternatively, that doing this project would be critical in helping us to reach our goal of more diverse leadership and also lead us into greater sustainability in our community. Thankfully, we were able to fund the website production through board leadership gifts and cost-savings in other areas. Northwestern University provided staff and financial support for the public launch of the project in March 2019. And our Hull House partnership was also funded with support from Northwestern and University of Illinois at Chicago, where Hull House is based.

There was additionally some board and leadership trepidation about taking on such a difficult project. There were lots of meetings where things were said like, "How much do we really have to talk about this?" and "Let's do this project and then it will be done and we can move on." Our entirely White board and staff needed to face their own feelings about race and their understanding of the history of racism in our country and community. We had to begin to come to terms with issues of race and racism ourselves, learn some history most of us had never really confronted, and decide where we stood individually and as a group.

Thankfully, we have recently added several Black leaders and scholars to our team and have benefited from their knowledge of this history. They have also provided some input on the best ways to approach these complicated issues and feedback on our work so far. Another factor is that talking about lynching itself is difficult, as the trauma of its violence surfaces even with mention of the word. A thoughtful sensitivity must be brought to any discussion in order for it to be productive rather than cause further damage.

Willard has often been portrayed, at the museum and in other ways, as a sainted leader who could do no wrong. Letting her be fully human, with failings and unmet challenges, was a new and controversial approach. Thankfully we could watch and learn from all of the many projects currently going on that take on revered historical leaders and their very real failings. We decided on some underlying principles to guide our work:

1. Historical figures are complicated and not perfect. It is important to examine them fully, to allow their imperfections to surface, and to try to learn from their mistakes.
2. Ultimately, it is up to each of us to decide, based on our own lenses of experience and views, the cultural worth of any historical figure.

By looking to the past for lessons in leadership issues and failures, we can find a realistic understanding of all of our limitations. We do this in the hopes of inspiring future leaders by creating a new kind of leadership model.

How do we reckon with historical figures who fought against one form of oppression (in Willard's case, the oppression of women) while shoring up others? We hope our work leads the public to explore this conflict for themselves and draw their own conclusions about Willard and her actions. In this way we can repair some of the damage she left behind and be leaders where Willard's leadership failed.

Notes

1. I want to acknowledge the great work of our initial group of Loyola University Chicago graduate students who got the project started and helped us to begin imagining what the final products might be. I also want to specifically thank Ella Wagner, who put in significant time and thought to this project. And, in addition to the board, council, and staff of the museum and archives, many people contributed to the overall project and numerous conversations helped us develop our approach and understanding. A full list of all partners, sponsors, and participants can be found on the website.
2. Frederick Douglass et al., to Frances Willard, "The Position of the National Woman's Christian Temperance Union of the United States in Relation to the Colored People," February 6, 1895, WCTU Archives, Evanston, IL.
3. Ida B. Wells, "Southern Horrors: Lynch Law in All Its Phases," in *Selected Works of Ida B. Wells-Barnett*, ed. Trudier Harris (New York: Oxford University Press, 1991), 17; "The Race Problem: Miss Willard on the Political Puzzle of the South," *Voice (New York)*, October 23, 1890; Ida B. Wells, "A Red Record: Tabulated Statistics and Alleged Causes of Lynchings in the United States, 1892–1893–1894," in Harris, *Selected Works*, 231.
4. "The Race Problem" (see note 2).

CHAPTER 8

Making Women's History More Visible

W HEN CONDUCTING RESEARCH FOR EXHIBITS and programs within the field of women's history, many practitioners find that their research leads to ambiguity rather than the definitive answers that they seek. Highlighting the accomplishments of women to make their stories more visible is a seemingly straightforward task that is often complicated by a lack of primary materials and a reliance on narrow research parameters. It is important, also, to be aware of our implicit biases. Archives and repositories typically offer relevant information on births, marriages, and deaths; however, there is not always enough data to fill in the blanks and to help build a compelling and gender-inclusive narrative for our visitors. This challenge becomes even more pronounced when searching for women's political activity, such as enfranchisement, citizenship, and voting rights from the past.[1] This chapter will address these challenges and also outline examples of more expansive and even creative research methods that can be replicated by practitioners and used widely to make women's history more visible.

Given the challenges to finding women's political voices in the past, it is not surprising that in many existing narratives women are typically portrayed as mere bystanders and not as active participants. As practitioners, we must continually challenge ourselves to think broadly about where and when women were present and the roles they played. Recognizing that gender bias is prevalent in our field, public historians Dr. Noelle Trent and Dr. Cindy Grisham offer guidance based on the challenges they faced when searching for a gender-inclusive narrative for their individual projects. One key practice they use is to proactively question their findings and revise their research parameters in recognition that the materials they were seeking might lay outside of a traditional research repository. To not do so can lead to accepting incomplete research data, resulting in an overly narrow and inaccurate historic interpretation.

In their work for the National Civil Rights Museum (NCRM) at the Lorraine Motel and the Arkansas Supreme Court Library, Dr. Noelle Trent and Dr. Cindy Grisham consciously recognize that women have always been part of the historic narrative. Although men's accomplishments have typically overshadowed contributions by women, their work as political activists amounts to more than that of just passive onlookers. In her role as the director of interpretation, exhibits, and programs at NCRM, Dr. Trent acknowledges the extent to which our biases can silently guide historical research and interpretation within public exhibitions and programs. Indeed, it is easy for visitors to walk away believing that women were not making major contributions when their names, photographs, and correspondence are traditionally absent from repositories, and are thus omitted from exhibits and public programs. The fact that men are typically some of the most celebrated and visible figures from the Civil Rights Movement, for example, could easily translate to exhibits built exclusively around a male narrative. The reality, however, is that while fewer women than men assumed public leadership roles, they still made lasting and significant contributions behind the scenes. Given this, Trent urges public historians "to be mindful of where we place women in our narrative; assume that they were right in the middle not just around the edges."[2]

During her tenure at the NCRM, Trent has made a concerted personal effort to ensure gender inclusivity in the organization's exhibits and programs. Her personal efforts are supported by their mission, which states "the major theme of the NCRM exhibitions, which emphasizes the role of ordinary people in ordinary times doing extraordinary things . . . which de-emphasizes the roles of major male leaders."[3] When beginning a new research project, Trent encourages public historians to constantly challenge the research findings, especially if they produce an overly male-centered storyline. She offers that her team embraces the following outlook: "In order to insure gender inclusivity even as we move forward in other exhibitions and programming ventures, we've retrained our eyes as practitioners." This deceivingly simple concept of retraining ourselves to pivot from the assumption that women were not present to one where *women were at the center of the activity* gives us the opportunity to creatively expand our research parameters and to construct a more accurate and inclusive historical narrative.

As a public service librarian, Grisham's work also demonstrates the importance of retraining ourselves to find women in new places. In her quest to discover the identity of an eighteenth-century woman in a small Arkansas community who donated the land to build a community church, Grisham also began with the assumption that there was more to the story than she initially found, leading her to develop a more creative research method. When the initial research yielded only the donor's name, despite the significant value of the land donation, Grisham, a genealogist and former police detective, felt compelled to discover more about this elusive donor.

To augment her historical research skills, Grisham relied heavily on the parallels that existed between her work in law enforcement and public history. Grisham notes that her approach to historical research is very similar to her career as a detective, and she encourages researchers to be unrelenting and even tenacious as they proceed with their historical research. Her process begins with recording all of the collected data on a large whiteboard and then constructing a timeline of key events. Next, she advises researchers to make a list of individuals who may have known or been associated with her subject: "You look for everyone around her. As a detective we called this the 'FAN,' for Family, Acquaintances, and Neighbors. It is common to find clues about your missing woman in the records of these individuals and they are usually going to be men."[4]

Ultimately, it took Grisham more than a year to piece together a comprehensive narrative about the land donor, who is now known as Martha Stalker. The difficulty in finding her identity was compounded by multiple barriers, including incorrect census records, which listed her name as "Stocker." Additional factors included Stalker's lack of formal education, which resulted in her inability to read or write, that she had been married and widowed three times, which resulted in children with different surnames, and that the property she owned was registered in her son-in-law's name. While any one of these details alone would have made Grisham's search difficult, the overlapping complexities of finding Stalker within the historical record initially resulted in multiple dead ends. Grisham's persistence and refusal to accept an incomplete history sheds an important new light on the lives and experiences of women in eighteenth-century Arkansas who have hitherto been overlooked. Similar to Trent, Grisham urges us to push back against the typical male-focused storyline, to actively question research results that appear inadequate, and to always begin with the assumption that women not only were present but also often played a key role in historical developments.

Useful Tips for Recovering Women's History

- Search both family and married names, keeping in mind the possibility of multiple marriages.
- Search for name-spelling variations.
- Look for male children and male siblings.
- Expand your search to the "FAN" network.
- Run parallel searches in neighboring towns, as jurisdictions, county lines, and local land boundaries change.
- Look for and explore inconsistencies in the data.

The challenge of searching for women's advocacy efforts for enfranchisement, citizenship, and voting rights is complicated not only by gender bias but also by institutional sexism and systemic racism as well. In the case study offered in chapter 9, history practitioner Rebecca Price shares the background behind the founding of her nonprofit organization, Chick History. Created specifically to "rebuild history one story at a time by focusing on women's history, educational programming, and community outreach," her work centers on expanding the narrative of women's enfranchisement.[5] When Price's initial research yielded insufficient information on African American women within the Tennessee women's suffrage movement, she questioned the findings. Instead of accepting the lack of sources as proof that African American women were not widely part of the political movement, she chose instead to assume that they were active, and that the repositories, which typically focused on the efforts of White women, were incomplete. To correct this misconception, Price launched a statewide community-based program exploring African American women's political contributions in Tennessee before 1930. When the project is completed, it will document, digitize, and make the missing women visible and ensure that their stories are chronicled alongside the efforts of White suffragists. In addition to providing both historians and the community access to important historic materials, it also showcases a project that can be implemented in other communities that face similar challenges.

Price's work demonstrates how a strong partnership with both the community and institutional support lead to a successful outcome. While the project was still in the developmental phase, Price reached out to Melissa Davis, director of community history programs with Humanities Tennessee, to share her ideas and garner feedback. Davis recalls that Price approached the project in two unique ways: First, Price reframed the general narrative of the suffrage movement from that of a celebratory story featuring only a handful of White icons to one that invited a more racially diverse set of participants. Equally important, Price also anticipated that the project would unfold at a slower pace, which ensured adequate time to make course corrections and facilitate a deeper connection with the local communities. This led Davis to characterize the project as a "win-win for both Humanities Tennessee and Chick History as it forged long-term relationships that will propel Price's work forward and help generate awareness of Humanities Tennessee at the same time."[6]

Price made multiple adjustments throughout the project and ensured that both the community and funder were aware of the modifications and expected outcomes. In one example, both Price and Davis realized that building the necessary relationships takes longer than a single grant cycle, and so built in a multi-year funding stream that gave the Chick History project team the ability to spend more time in the communities. This slower pace allowed the local participants to have a voice in how their stories were told as well as be trained to digitize the materials themselves, instead of relying solely on the outside project team. This ensured that all participants felt vested in the project, which contributed to its overall success.

Working closely with members of the community and funders has many benefits, including the potential to reshape projects. Being open to collaboration and exploring new ideas throughout the work process can also shine a light into areas that need a more nuanced or careful approach. For example, when the Chick History project team began to receive feedback from members of the community, they realized they needed to make a course correction by asking different questions in order to find sources about the local African American women who campaigned for suffrage.

Unlike many White women in the movement, or African American women in the Northeast, African American women in the South did not always self-identify as suffragists or even as working for a political cause.[7] Armed with this knowledge, the project team altered their research parameters to include looking for women who described their work as focusing on the betterment of their families and communities as well as securing an education for their children. Their efforts crossed into multiple areas, and they began to look for women who worked through local churches, women's clubs, and sororities. As a result, they ultimately found women whose work also included suffrage.[8]

Had the project team not reframed the search parameters and begun asking more pertinent questions, the results could have been vastly different and more limited. While the Chick History project has a specific content focus, the results show that abandoning a predetermined research plan, and instead adopting a more analytical and creative approach, can add significant value to the outcomes, and can be widely replicated by others.

If we are to fulfill our goal of making women's history more visible, then we need to change the way we approach our work. The lack of resources available in archives and repositories is not unique to women's political history; to the contrary, it is a systemic issue within the larger women's history field that will not be corrected quickly. Therefore, as we move forward to interpret and expand the narrative of women's political activism, we should strive to emulate the work of practitioners such as Noelle Trent, Cindy Grisham, and Rebecca Price. Using their work as models, we should retrain ourselves to recognize implicit biases, assume that women were part of the storyline even when facing ambiguous research results, and think creatively about the questions that guide our work. If successful, then the work at our museums and historic sites will serve to facilitate contemporary conversations around race, gender, intersectionality, and equality, which will not only benefit our individual work, or institution, but also advance our field as well.

Notes

1. American Association for State and Local History, "2020 AASLH Suffrage Value Statement Call for Public Comment" (unpublished Online Field Survey, October 2018).
2. Noelle Trent, email correspondence with author, February 2019.
3. Trent, email correspondence with author.
4. Cindy Grisham, email correspondence with author, November 2018–February 2019.
5. "Our History," Chick History, accessed June 2018, https://chickhistory.org/about-2.
6. Melissa Davis, phone interview with author, July 28, 2018.
7. Elna C. Green, *Southern Strategies: Southern Women and the Woman Suffrage Question* (Chapel Hill: University of North Carolina Press, 1997), 26.
8. For a deeper look into African American women's participation in political activism, see Rosalyn Terborg-Penn, *African American Women in the Struggle for the Vote, 1850–1920* (Bloomington: Indiana University Press, 1998); Ann D. Gordon and Bettye Collier-Thomas, eds., *African American Women and the Vote: 1837 to 1965* (Amherst: University of Massachusetts Press, 1997); Marjorie Spruill Wheeler, *New Women of the New South: The Leaders of the Women's Suffrage Movement in the Southern United States* (New York: Oxford University Press, 1993); Paula Giddings, *Ida: A Sword Among Lions; Ida B. Wells and the Campaign Against Lynching* (New York: Amistad, 2009); and Lorraine Gates Schuyler, *The Weight of Their Votes: Southern Women and Political Leverage in the 1920s* (Chapel Hill: University of North Carolina Press, 2006).

CHAPTER 9

Protecting the Legacy

Documenting and Digitizing African American Women's Political History Prior to 1930

Rebecca Price

WHEN I ENTERED THE MUSEUM FIELD in the late 1990s, we were at the beginning of a new trend in historical interpretation with an emphasis on "voices." Graduate programs and museums at the forefront encouraged interpretation to include all of the voices, from the men, to the women, to the servants, to the enslaved, and so on. It was an exciting time because there was a seemingly unified effort to make sure more people were represented in the narrative.

However, as my career progressed, I began to struggle with the field's interpretation of historical events involving women, and with the presentation of women's history in general. I was excited to hear more voices, but I became concerned about the narrative surrounding those voices. While women were mentioned, they were taking on supportive roles, they were tucked away in the corner of a permanent exhibit, or they were watered-down. We had the "who" but now we need to focus on the "how." More to the point: How are we telling the stories of women?

I founded Chick History to begin tackling these issues head on. I took what was once a part-time blog called *Chick History* that I began in 2010, and I incorporated it as a non-profit in 2015. Our mission is to rebuild history one story at a time by focusing on women's history, educational programming, and community outreach. Chick History is committed to preserving and interpreting all women's histories and experiences through its unique programs, community-driven projects, and strategic partnerships.

"March to the 19th"

In 2016, Chick History launched "March to the 19th"—in partnership with Humanities Tennessee—a grassroots campaign for women's history leading up to 2020 and the centennial celebration of the Nineteenth Amendment. Since launching, we've been traveling across Tennessee and engaging with various audiences to achieve our goals for this campaign and address some critical needs for women's history, such as professional development and educational resources.

In 2017, we began a phase called "Protecting the Legacy." Together with a coalition of history partners across the state, we are digitizing family and local history related to African American women's political history in Tennessee before 1930. This is an effort to expand the narrative of suffrage, voting, and political activity and to preserve the contributions and experiences of African American women during this time period in Tennessee. At a series of "digitization events" being held across the state, we are asking the public to bring in family and community history to be digitized and preserved.

Figure 9.1.   Dr. Earnestine Jenkins, left, takes notes and listens while Hattie Yarbrough, right, talks about her aunt, Annie Sybil Thomas Jarret. Mrs. Yarbrough was among participants who brought in family photographs and letters to the November 2017 Chick History Digitization Event at the National Civil Rights Museum in Memphis. Among the material she brought in was a studio portrait of her aunt taken by James P. Newton, the first black professional photographer in Memphis whose work is extremely rare. Image courtesy of Chick History

Documenting the Political Activity of African American Women

How to document the political activity of African American Women is the driving question behind "Protecting the Legacy," and a statewide task force spent almost a year discussing and creating a collection methodology and subject matter scope to answer it. Much of the conversation centered around the fact that if the project focused specifically on suffrage, the many ways in which African American women were politically active during segregation would be missed.

One of the very first things we talked about was the limitation of the word *suffrage* in the context of African American women's history. If we stick to the traditional objective—"find material on suffrage and Black women"—we will not be very successful. If we focused only on finding information related to the passage of suffrage, we would miss all of the other ways that African American women influenced the vote or engaged in political activity from their perspective. So that's the question we've chosen to ask: How do you show the political activity of African American women? Thus, instead of looking for suffrage, we are focusing on activism in order to explore the political activity of African American women.

It was also important for the project team that segregation was our starting point, not the end point. As Dr. Earnestine Jenkins—a professor of art history in the Department of Art at the University of Memphis and the lead humanities scholar for "Protecting the Legacy"—says, "The traditional narrative does often leave out large groups of women who don't fit into the white, middle-class story of women's rights. You have to be honest about the racism in the movement and the extent they kept women of color out of the movement. . . . You have to look for those hidden histories because, otherwise, you are not going to get it."[1] For the project, this approach means looking for old newspapers or church programs with meeting notices for the local chapters of the National Association of Colored Women's Clubs. It means digging through old photographs for pictures of women who were active in the community and church. It means looking differently at letters, journals, or everyday material long stashed away in an attic, and rethinking the sense of community history, and what it means for an African American woman to be politically active during that time period.

Portrait of Annie Sybil Thomas Jarret, ca. 1900

A perfect example of the type of success we've had when we change the definition, and therefore expand the narrative, is the *Portrait of Annie Sybil Thomas Jarret.* The first digitization event, held at the National Civil Rights Museum in Memphis, Tennessee, in November 2017, yielded a new archive of dozens of items, including interviews with several African American women in their mid-nineties. Among the rare and important findings is a studio portrait of Annie Sybil Thomas Jarret taken by pioneering photographer James P. Newton, the first professional Black photographer in Memphis, who operated a studio on Beale Street. Newton photographs are extremely rare, and this portrait of Annie Jarret is just one of the ways in which African American women expressed political activity. Annie Sybil Thomas Jarret was an educator and among the first generation of African American woman voters in Tennessee. Imagery played a critical role in crafting the visual stereo-

Figure 9.2.   Studio Portrait of Annie Sybil Thomas Jarret taken by James P. Newton around 1900 in Memphis, Tennessee. Newtown was the first professional Black photographer in Memphis. Jarret was a teacher born near Saulsbury, Tennessee, who left a legacy to her family of the importance of education, civic engagement, and the contributions of African Americans to history. Jarret is among the first generation of African American women voters in Tennessee. Image courtesy of Chick History

types that developed alongside the rise of segregation and racial subordination. To counter politically motivated racist imagery, photographers such as Newton were central to visually documenting the achievements of Black Americans such as Jarret and transforming the visual representation of African Americans as they strived for full citizenship and political enfranchisement.[2]

Using Critical Race Theory in Historical Perseveration Methodology

A crucial element of the project was making sure the process and the final collection reflected elements of Critical Race Theory (CRT). As mentioned, the task force and committee members were already cognizant that we did not want to embark on a project that ended with segregation as the final narrative. Dr. Jenkins pointed out early on the limitations of focusing solely on the traditional historical definition of *suffrage*. In order to authentically capture the experiences of African American women during this time period, and to truly expand our understanding, we were going to have to critically listen to our audience and the women we were working with. What did they have to say about themselves, their families, and their histories? What did they define as political activity? What did they say was important? What was history to their family and community?

Additionally, we wanted to ensure our participants that it was their words and their voices that we would document, not our interpretation of their lived experiences. Throughout the project, from spokespeople to the stories we captured, African American women are centered as the authority on this narrative and the keepers of this history. The majority of all our partners and advisors, and the community groups we work with, are led by African American women.

Although these were some of the project's core values from the very beginning, it was not until attending a session at the 2018 AASLH Annual Meeting in Kansas City on CRT that I was able to place some of these practices in a professional framework.[3] Accordingly, "Protecting the Legacy" endeavored to:

- create experiences that dismantle racism instead of putting it on display;
- encourage diverse narratives that benefit people of color without having to appeal to the interest of Whites;
- move away from narratives as told through the eyes of the oppressor; and
- allow African American women to question the dominant narrative and be seen as a credible voice for their own experiences.

One example of this in practice involved an oral history participant who was one of the Nashville Freedom Riders. She is frequently asked to speak on this experience, which she confessed gives her great anxiety because she relives the trauma every time she tells it. For "Protecting the Legacy," our oral history coordinator assured her that we did want to speak about that event in her life, but also wanted to talk to her about her mother and grandmother, and so on, and the women who came before her and influenced her. In this way, she did not have to "put on display" via an oral history the racism that led to the Freedom Rides, and instead was able to speak about her family and influences that led her to be a civil rights participant who worked to dismantle racism.

The Process Becomes the Project

As the project progressed, we soon discovered that equally important to the digital collection, and maybe even more so, was the journey that would lead us to that final product. As another museum who embarked on a long-term, community-driven project noted:

> [The] exhibitions were not the product; they were a means to interact with and learn from and about the community. They were a part of the process in community engagement. Exhibits were not just showpieces, but part of a programmatic toolkit to foster trust and learning in a community.[4]

We also understood that every interaction we had with a participant was a way to personally serve them. Although we initially identified the educators and the public who would access the collection as the primary benefactors, we realized that every time we interacted with a participant, we engaged and fulfilled our mission.

Filling a Void in the Archives

The final destination for this collection will be a public archive. We finished the collection and digitization process in November 2018 and will spend the majority of 2019 and 2020 processing and editing the data. Once this is complete, the entire collection will be donated to the Special Collections Center at the Nashville Public Library. From there, it will become available to the public for educational and research purposes.

We hope that what makes this digital collection unique, and what we hope can serve as a model for other organizations, is that these historical records will come with the history attached. When there is a void in the archives, someone else comes along and tells your story for you. With this project, we've let the women speak for themselves and tell their own story. Put best by one of the Knoxville participants: "We have the opportunity to write our history, make our history, and to share our history . . . so we cannot blame anyone if we don't tell our story."

Notes

1. Jessica Bliss, "Chick History Wants to Uncover Black Women's Suffrage Stories in Tennessee," *The Tennessean*, January 22, 2017, www.tennessean.com/story/life/2017/01/22/chick-history-wants-uncover-black-womens-suffrage-stories-tennessee/96498576.
2. Earnestine Jenkins, "Portrait of Annie Sybil Thomas Jarret by James P. Newton—First Black Professional Photographer in Memphis," *Chick History*, February 27, 2018, www.protect.chickhistory.org/2018/02/27/portrait-of-annie-sybil-thomas-jarret-chick-history.
3. Dina Bailey, Melanie Adams, and Lauren Zalut, "Racism: Is Your Museum Ready to Talk about It?" American Association for State and Local History Annual Meeting, Kansas City, MO, September 28, 2018.
4. Kate Baillion, Janeen Bryant, and Kamille Bostick, "Failing Forward: ¡NUEVOlution! Latinos and the New South," *History News* 73, no. 3 (Summer 2018): 15.

CHAPTER 10

Inviting New Perspectives through Community Dialogue

THE PRECEDING CHAPTERS HAVE ADVOCATED for practitioners to take a deeper look at women's involvement in political actions such as work toward enfranchisement and voting rights in order to share a more accurate historical narrative with the public. To do so requires that practitioners reevaluate and broaden their research methods in order to allow the previously untold stories to reemerge and take their place alongside the more celebrated narratives. As part of this process, we must also acknowledge the systemic racism within our organizations that have allowed the more abbreviated and exclusive narratives to determine public programs and exhibition content.

That said, simply identifying that racism and biases exist will not correct the deeper divisions nor repair any previous insensitive interpretations. In order to undertake the next phase of this work, an early critical component is to convene conversations that allow participants to jointly consider different perspectives, explore systemic racism, ask new questions, and come away with a deeper understanding of the needs of both the organization and the community. This process is neither easy nor fast, but making it an early priority will ultimately set the stage for more inclusive and vibrant programs that are relevant for the overall community in the long run.

Looking again at the case studies, the FWHM took the boldest approach in confronting their history of racism as they chose to put forward a candid and undiluted dialogue about Frances Willard. This examination openly explored the conflict and well-known animosity between Ida B. Wells and Willard without interpretation or editing by the staff, and ultimately documented this work on a website replete with educational resources. By inviting the public to become part of the conversation through events and public forums, they allowed a deeper and more compelling story to unfold, one that resonated with their visitors and the public.

By contrast, the NWP took a careful approach and began to cautiously explore the organization's history of systemic racism during a series of focus groups in 2017.[1] The main goal was to explore the ongoing relevance of an organization that had been founded more than one hundred years earlier and whose political gravitas had flailed after the 1970s. Like many small organizations, the NWP did not have the funding to engage a focus-group facilitator. Fortunately, the NWP was able to rely on a former board member whose work centered on group dynamics and so provided in-kind support. While this allowed them to begin the process, financial resources did not allow for an adequate and diverse sampling of participants, as most professional pollsters compensate their participants. Instead, they relied on direct outreach by board members and staff to issue invitations and build the discussion groups. While not ideal, the conversations did act as a catalyst to introduce the history to an expanded audience and allowed them to begin exploring the more contentious aspects of the history.

The NWP had long resisted delving in to the racist allegations against party leadership and so even the first step of convening focus groups required weighing the positive and negative ramifications of their actions. The NWP is not unique in that they took a more cautious approach; given that operating small historic sites and museums is often complicated by both financial and governance issues, delving into institutional racism can be exceptionally problematic. In fact, it is not uncommon for organizations to avoid, or at least to postpone, such work until they have a high level of support from staff, volunteers, and board members. To push back on this, nonprofit professional Janedra Sykes believes that avoiding or delaying this important work could actually be more detrimental than taking a direct approach. She cautions, "Whether we realize it or not, the work is happening informally. . . . You may not be having the conversations within your organizations, but on another level the greater community is. . . . The question becomes, do you want to more proactively help shape that conversation?"[2] Sykes is correct; if we fail to engage in robust conversations, then we have lost the opportunity to receive valuable feedback from the community.

Finding opportunities to hold critical conversations fosters an environment of productive collaboration between organizations and their community. While many museums and historic sites routinely offer interactive exhibits, tours, and program content, these efforts are still lacking. At best these methods often provide only a passive way for the audience to participate after the content has already been developed and vetted by staff. As we learned from both the FWHM and Chick History case studies, it is the critical and ongoing community conversations held *during the early developmental phase of the work* that ultimately increased the overarching value of each project. By inviting the public to become early thought partners during the process of writing a narrative and producing programs and exhibits and not just consumers of the final work product, they were able to make nimble course corrections in real time and successfully facilitate conversations within their organizations.

What to Consider Before Convening a Community Dialogue

There are multiple ways to engage with communities and begin an exploratory dialogue. Formal focus groups, public programs that include a heavy Q&A segment, or even launching a survey are all common tools used by historic sites and museums. Depending on the needs of the organization and the level of staff and financial resources, any of these options can be an effective way to gain the public perspective. However, before moving forward, each organization should carefully consider how staff and the board would participate. If the overarching goal is to learn new and unbiased information and not simply to repeat past conversations, then direct participation by staff and the board may be unnecessary and may even impede the work. If this is the case, then consider convening separate internal discussions to ensure that staff and board members' participation adds value.

Smaller organizations can also consider partnering with other organizations, neighborhood groups, or local collaboratives to jointly convene discussion groups. Partnering on these efforts allows for sharing the administrative burden, guarantees a broader spectrum of participants, and also ensures that the conversation does not focus solely on the needs of the individual organization. Instead, the conversation will concentrate on learning from the participants and gaining an understanding of the needs of the larger community.

Given that the history of women's rights in America is often included in conversations that center on contemporary politics, it is not surprising that museums and practitioners face having their work criticized as "too political."[3] Thus convening conversations around voting rights, women's equality, and racism may bring unintended negative attention. Despite this, the need to hold these conversations is more critical than ever, and there are ways to mitigate any adverse reactions. Sykes promotes using a "tone of historical review, with the overarching theme that as Americans we've been in contentious times before and have been able to move the country forward."[4] By refocusing the narrative from politics to one centered on the importance of civic engagement and advocacy, the focus shifts to a topic that is perceived as less confrontational. This allows the conversation to become a productive dialogue and not be dismissed as an overly divisive or partisan message.

For the organization that chooses to foster an environment of productive collaboration with their community, the next step is to find or develop a model that fits their individual needs. The International Coalition of Sites of Conscience offers a valuable guide as it takes into consideration financial limits, provides an accurate and sufficient historic background, and effectively shifts the focus from partisan politics to civic engagement. Developed as part of the larger series of front-page dialogues that cover critical social justice topics such as "Guns in America," "Museums and Me Too," and "Women's Rights," the "Voting Rights Discussion Guide" is an important resource for organizations moving forward to convene critical conversations.[5]

Voting Rights Discussion Guide

The guide is an easy-to-use tool that concisely lays out a roadmap to guide a community forum centered on voting rights and political engagement. The guide is written so that either a professional facilitator or a moderator can lead the process, which makes it equally usable for museums of all sizes. If resources allow, it is ideal to record the sessions and then engage someone to transcribe the dialogue, or at a minimum designate someone to act as the official scribe. Either option allows for the material to be shared quickly and provides an accurate record of the sessions. The "Voting Rights Discussion Guide" queues up the conversation by first presenting the historical narrative, in this case using a series of historic quotes centering on women's suffrage. By providing the historical narrative first, this allows

FRONT PAGE DIALOGUE

Voting Rights

Passed in 1920, the 19th Amendment to the US Constitution secured the right to vote for women in America. Despite this, women of color faced state and local restrictions to exercising their vote freely, and many at the time noted that all women still had a long way to go to obtain equality where voting and equal rights were concerned." After the Amendment passed, women's rights advocate Alice Paul said, "It is incredible to me that any woman should consider the fight for full equality won. It has just begun." As the 100th anniversary of the Amendment approaches, inequitable access to voting – among other things – remains a key issue for many marginalized groups, especially African American women and men. Debates over voter registration guidelines, gerrymandering, election monitoring, and the geographic location of polling centers are frequently heated and the sources of deep tension in communities across the country.

Voting can be an empowering assertion of voice, right and identity; but in practice it can also be an exclusionary and diminishing process where hierarchies are reinforced and power concentrated. Since 1920, several laws have passed that have alternately strengthened and weakened equal access to voting. For instance, while the Voting Rights Act of 1965 prohibited racial discrimination in voting, a 2013 Supreme Court ruling left states in charge of their own voting registration procedures with no requirement that they prove those procedures are equitable. This has enabled states to pass laws – surrounding new identification requirements and polling access, for example – that have negatively and disproportionately affected communities of color. In addition to race, literacy, gender, age, ethnicity and the existence of a criminal record all continue to be factors leveraged to shrink the voting power of traditionally disenfranchised groups, setting people at odds with each other.

As a result, six million Americans are currently forbidden to vote because of prior felony convictions alone – a disproportionate number of them people of color. Some states are cutting back, or eliminating, early voting which most impacts low income earners, who work more often for hourly wages. Further, the ACLU estimates that one in five people eligible to vote has a disability. While the Americans with Disabilities Act requires every polling center to have staff that can assist disabled voters, this is not always equally enforced. Finally, while women have fought for the right to vote throughout most of the 20th century, universal suffrage was only had in 2015 – when Saudi Arabia became the last country to allow women to vote. Despite this, many women across the globe endure violence and threats when voting today.

As we continue to redefine the right to vote, Sites of Conscience have an important role to play in facilitating constructive conversations and creating spaces where visitors, particularly those who may not always agree, listen to each other in new ways. Below is one model for engaging visitors in dialogue around voting rights. We encourage you to adapt and ground the dialogue in the unique history that your Site of Conscience works to preserve and share.

©The International Coalition of Sites of Conscience, a global network of historic sites, museums and memory initiatives connecting past struggles to today's movements for human rights and social Justice To learn more about the Coalition methodology and dialogue Sarah Pharaon (spharaon @sitesofconscience.org), Dina Bailey (dbailey@sitesofconscience.org) or Braden Paynter (bpaynter@sitesofconscience.org).

Figure 10.1.   International Coalition of Sites of Conscience Voting Rights Guide. International Coalition of Sites of Conscience https://www.sitesofconscience.org/en/resources/frontpagedialogues

International Coalition of
SITES *of* **CONSCIENCE**

HOW TO USE FRONT PAGE DIALOGUES

Rather than using all the model questions suggested under each phase, facilitators may select questions that reflect the evolving conversation of the group they are guiding in dialogue. Some questions may be useful for multiple topics; we mark these with slashes (ex. gender/race/activism). Finally, we are always available to work with you as you develop your dialogue session. If you are not familiar with the Arc of Dialogue model, you can contact our team at training@sitesofconscience.org for support and more information.

GUIDELINES

What are the group agreements or guidelines for the dialogue that help us establish the "container" that the dialogue occurs within? Here are some sample agreements:

1.   Share the air: leave room for everyone to speak.
2.   Our unique backgrounds and social status give us different life experiences.
3.   Seek first to understand—ask questions to clarify, not to debate.

PREPARATION

Facilitator should adhere enlarged versions of the quotes listed as Shared Content around the dialogue space.

SITES OF CONSCIENCE MEMBERS WHO CAN BE RESOURCES FOR YOUR EFFORTS

•   Matilda Joslyn Gage Foundation
•   Women's Rights National Historic Park
•   Lowell National Historic Park
•   Museum of Women's Resistance

SHARED CONTENT:

"I do not think the mere extension of the ballot a panacea for all the ills of our national life. What we need today is not simply more voters, but better voters. — Frances Ellen Watkins Harper

"We have been holding conventions for years – we have been assembling together and whining over our difficulties and afflictions, passing resolutions on resolutions to any extent," she wrote. "But it does really seem that we have made but little progress considering our resolves." — Mary Ann Shad Cary

"And so, lifting as we climb, onward and upward we go, struggling and striving, and hoping that the buds and blossoms of our desires will burst into glorious fruition ere long. With courage, born of success achieved in the past, with a keen sense of the responsibility, which we shall continue to assume, we look forward to a future large with promise and hope. Seeking no favors because of our color, nor patronage because of our needs, we knock at the bar of justice, asking an equal chance." — Mary Church Terrell

"Think of Patrick and Sambo and Hans and Yung Tung who do not know the difference between a monarchy and a republic, who never read the Declaration of Independence or Webster's spelling book, making laws for Lydia Maria Childs, Lucretia Mott, or Fanny Kemble." — Elizabeth Cady Stanton

Frederick Douglass: ...I must say that I do not see how any one can pretend that there is the same urgency in giving the ballot to woman as to the negro. With us, the matter is a question of life and death... When women, because they are women, are hunted down through the cities of New York and New Orleans; when they are dragged from their houses and hung upon lamp-posts... when their children are not allowed to enter schools; then they will have an urgency to obtain the ballot equal to our own. (Great applause.)

A Voice: Is that not all true about black women?

©The International Coalition of Sites of Conscience, a global network of historic sites, museums and memory initiatives connecting past struggles to today's movements for human rights and social justice. To learn more about the Coalition methodology and dialogue Sarah Pharaon (spharaon@sitesofconscience.org), Lara Bailey (lbailey@sitesofconscience.org), or Braden Paynter (bpaynter@sitesofconscience.org).

Figure 10.2.   International Coalition of Sites of Conscience Voting Rights Guide. International Coalition of Sites of Conscience https://www.sitesofconscience.org/en/resources/frontpagedialogues

Mr. Douglass: Yes, yes, yes; it is true of the black woman, but not because she is a woman, but because she is black. (Applause.) ...

Susan B. Anthony: The old anti-slavery school say women must stand back and wait until the negroes shall be recognized. But we say, if you will not give the whole loaf of suffrage to the entire people, give it to the most intelligent first. (Applause.) If intelligence, justice, and morality are to have precedence in the Government, let the question of woman be brought up first and that of the negro last. (Applause.)... When Mr. Douglass mentioned the black man first and the woman last, if he had noticed he would have seen that it was the men that clapped and not the women. There is not a woman born who desires to eat the bread of dependence, no matter whether it be from the hand of father, husband, or brother; for any one who does so eat her bread places herself in the power of the person from whom she takes it. (Applause.) Mr. Douglass talks about the wrongs of the negro; but with all the outrages that he to-day suffers, he would not exchange his sex and take the place of Elizabeth Cady Stanton. (Laughter and applause.) https://archive.org/stream/historyofwomansu02stanuoft#page/382/mode/2up history of women's suffrage

Nine percent of black respondents and 9 percent of Hispanic respondents indicated that, in the last election, they (or someone in their household) were told that they lacked the proper identification to vote. Just 3 percent of whites said the same. Ten percent of black respondents and 11 percent of Hispanic respondents reported that they were incorrectly told that they weren't listed on voter rolls, as opposed to 5 percent of white respondents. Only 27 percent of white Americans say that eligible voters being denied the right to vote is a major problem today, and you have really strong majorities of black and Hispanic Americans—six in 10, roughly—saying that it is a major concern. – *The Atlantic* https://www.theatlantic.com/politics/archive/2018/07/poll-prri-voter-suppression/565355/

...37 percent of white respondents reported that their parents had taken them to a voting booth when they were children, versus 24 percent of black respondents and 18 percent of Hispanics. In a region where, because of Jim Crow, many middle-aged or older people of color may not have had a parent who was even eligible to vote during their childhood, voting simply isn't as established an intergenerational civic institution as it is in white communities—even as it faces new threats today. — *The Atlantic* https://www.theatlantic.com/politics/archive/2018/07/poll-prri-voter-suppression/565355/

In 2018, the Brennan Center's Voting Laws Roundup shows that lawmakers in eight states have introduced at least 16 bills making it harder to vote, and 35 restrictive bills in 14 states have carried over from previous legislative sessions. If passed, the laws would increase restrictions on voter registration and limit early and absentee voting opportunities, among other changes. https://www.brennancenter.org/press-release/new-analysis-voter-suppression-laws-concern-2018-though-many-states-looking-expand

©The International Coalition of Sites of Conscience, a global network of historic sites, museums and memory initiatives connecting past struggles to today's movements for human rights and social Justice. To learn more about the Coalition methodology and dialogue Sarah Pharaon (spharaon @sitesofconscience.org), Dina Bailey (dbailey@sitesofconscience.org) or Braden Paynter (bpaynter@sitesofconscience.org).

Figure 10.3.   International Coalition of Sites of Conscience Voting Rights Guide. International Coalition of Sites of Conscience https://www.sitesofconscience.org/en/resources/frontpagedialogues

PHASE I - COMMUNITY BUILDING

Questions in Phase 1 help build the "learning community" and break down artificial barriers between people by allowing participants to share information about themselves.

Facilitator should welcome the group, introduce themselves, explain their role, and explain the purpose of the dialogue. Facilitator should also ask for agreement to the guidelines established for the group.

> Who is a woman in your life you respect? How did their life experiences shape how you view "women's rights"?

> Share a story of an act of resistance you witnessed or participated in.

> What was your first voting experience?

> Who or what first taught you about politics and what did you learn?

PHASE II - SHARING OUR OWN EXPERIENCES

Questions in Phase 2 help participants recognize how their experiences are alike and different and why.

Facilitator should invite participants to move around the space and read all of the quotes, silently. After reading, participants are instructed to stand near the quote that they would like to speak more about. Participants are then encouraged to discuss why they chose that quote within their small group before returning to the large group to explore any of the following:

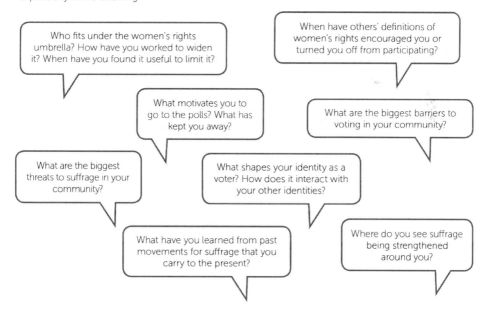

> Who fits under the women's rights umbrella? How have you worked to widen it? When have you found it useful to limit it?

> When have others' definitions of women's rights encouraged you or turned you off from participating?

> What motivates you to go to the polls? What has kept you away?

> What are the biggest barriers to voting in your community?

> What are the biggest threats to suffrage in your community?

> What shapes your identity as a voter? How does it interact with your other identities?

> What have you learned from past movements for suffrage that you carry to the present?

> Where do you see suffrage being strengthened around you?

Figure 10.4.   International Coalition of Sites of Conscience Voting Rights Guide. International Coalition of Sites of Conscience https://www.sitesofconscience.org/en/resources/frontpagedialogues

International Coalition of
SITES of CONSCIENCE

PHASE III - EXPLORING BEYOND OURSELVES
Questions in Phase 3 help participants engage in inquiry and exploration about the dialogue topic in an effort to learn with and from one another.

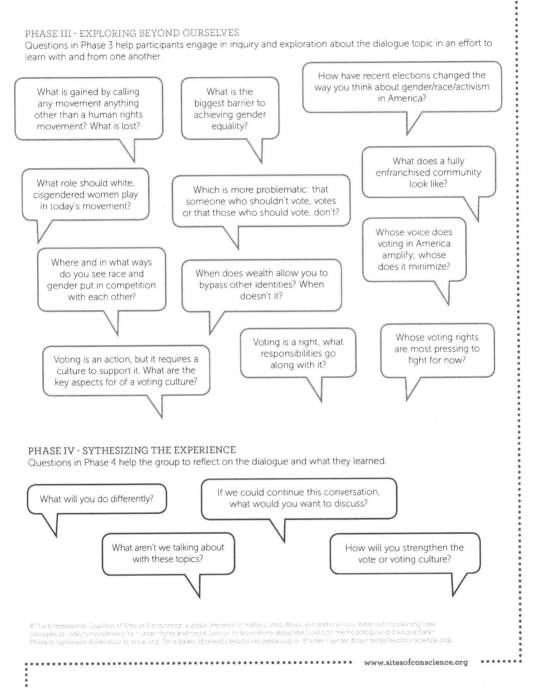

What is gained by calling any movement anything other than a human rights movement? What is lost?

What is the biggest barrier to achieving gender equality?

How have recent elections changed the way you think about gender/race/activism in America?

What role should white, cisgendered women play in today's movement?

Which is more problematic: that someone who shouldn't vote, votes or that those who should vote, don't?

What does a fully enfranchised community look like?

Where and in what ways do you see race and gender put in competition with each other?

When does wealth allow you to bypass other identities? When doesn't it?

Whose voice does voting in America amplify; whose does it minimize?

Voting is an action, but it requires a culture to support it. What are the key aspects for of a voting culture?

Voting is a right, what responsibilities go along with it?

Whose voting rights are most pressing to fight for now?

PHASE IV - SYTHESIZING THE EXPERIENCE
Questions in Phase 4 help the group to reflect on the dialogue and what they learned.

What will you do differently?

If we could continue this conversation, what would you want to discuss?

What aren't we talking about with these topics?

How will you strengthen the vote or voting culture?

www.sitesofconscience.org

Figure 10.5. International Coalition of Sites of Conscience Voting Rights Guide. International Coalition of Sites of Conscience https://www.sitesofconscience.org/en/resources/frontpagedialogues

all the participants to start the conversation with the same level of knowledge and understanding. Thus, the conversation will evolve and unfold based on who is in the room along with their beliefs around politics, gender, and race.

The guide defines four distinct phases for group participation. Building on the historic narrative, phase 1 offers sample questions such as "What was your first voting experience?" that allow the group to learn more about each other as individuals and find common ground. Phase 2 delves deeper through an interactive exercise where participants react to a series of questions posed to prompt personal reflection and understanding. Once the participants have become more familiar with each other, and themselves, phase 3 dives deeper into systemic racism and how we think about race through a series of exploratory questions such as "What role should White, cisgendered women play in today's movement?" In phase 4, the group can reflect on the overall dialogue and discuss the ways the process has changed or expanded their viewpoint on voting rights and women's involvement in political actions.

For those museums and historic sites working to expand their historical narratives, and to repair past insensitive interpretations, convening public conversations early in the process provides an opportunity to develop and present more accurate and compelling content within their programs and exhibits. Ultimately, this allows a better understanding of how the uneven application of women's enfranchisement continues to impact our nation politically, and why intersectionality remains critical to address. Race, gender, religion, politics, and class bias will continue to divide our communities until we unlearn what we think we know about this history and begin to facilitate contemporary conversations around the full breadth of women's equality.

Notes

1. Page Harrington, unpublished focus group notes, National Woman's Party, Washington, DC, October 2017.
2. Janedra Sykes, "We Need to Talk," interview by author, *There's No Crying in Women's History* (blog), June 5, 2020, www.pageharrington.com/blog.
3. American Association for State and Local History, "2020 AASLH Suffrage Value Statement Call for Public Comment," unpublished online field survey, October 2018.
4. Sykes, "We Need to Talk" (see note 2).
5. "Front Page Dialogues," International Coalition of Sites of Conscience, accessed August 31, 2020, www.sitesofconscience.org/en/resources/frontpagedialogues.

CHAPTER 11

The New Legacy of Suffrage

B Y 2010 I HAD BEEN THE EXECUTIVE DIRECTOR of Sewall-Belmont House and Museum for two years, and while the economic upheaval of the Great Recession had begun to level off, like many small museums, SBHM was still not financially sustainable. That said, an uptick in donations and grant income allowed for a new full-time staff position. The membership and development manager would lead donor relations and membership campaigns, and execute fundraising events. SBHM welcomed Chitra Panjabi to fill the post, a recent graduate from George Washington University with an MA in women's studies. A self-described feminist and political activist, her nascent interest in women's suffrage grew as she learned more about NWP and their place in the U.S. suffrage movement. Her role included giving museum tours to potential donors and writing fundraising collateral materials; both tasks required a strong understanding of the history and relevance of the NWP. Panjabi both excelled at and enjoyed the work, later sharing with me that the suffragists' stories resonated with her largely due to her belief in self-determination and political autonomy for women.

Ms. Panjabi was routinely surprised at the lack of knowledge around American political history, especially the women's suffrage movement. She also recognized that as the sole woman of color on staff at the time, she viewed the history and exhibits through a different lens than the rest of staff. An exhibit text panel in a first-floor gallery that illustrated the post–Nineteenth Amendment political role of women of color spoke of the women only in terms of being the "first" to hold an office. There was no analysis of the far-reaching accomplishments of women such as Shirley Chisholm and Patsy Mink.[1] This oversight was not lost on Panjabi. As a woman of color, she had to navigate the tension between being included in the small circle of professional staff charged with advancing the mission, and yet excluded, as the exhibits' narratives were largely silent about women of color. This was certainly a burden that the rest of the staff did not carry.

Panjabi left SBHM after a few years, and by 2015 she had completed the requirements to become a U.S. citizen. Later that year, she penned "Becoming American," a blog post for SBHM in which she recounted the barriers to political participation growing up in post-handover Hong Kong, her excitement as she looked forward to casting her first vote as an American citizen, and her experience at SBHM. She also recognized that if she had been "a contemporary of Alice [Paul] and Lucy's [Burns] I might have been pushed aside during the campaign [for suffrage] instead of embraced."[2] Given that the NWP was predominantly comprised of White women, Ms. Panjabi's assumption is more than likely accurate. That said her understanding and acceptance of the deeply nuanced history of women's suffrage and her place within it is a notable example for history practitioners.

Figure 11.1.   Chitra Panjabi introducing President Obama during the designation. Photo by Haley Harrington

On April 12, 2016, President Barack Obama utilized the American Antiquities Act of 1906 and designated the Sewall-Belmont House and Museum as a National Monument. As the Belmont-Paul Women's Equality National Monument (BEPA), it is the only monument recognized for women's equality and the first named for two women.[3] During the substantial preparation for the designation ceremony, a White House aide read Panjabi's blog post and invited her to introduce President Obama at the event. While the significance of witnessing a recently naturalized citizen and a woman of color introduce the president may have been lost on some, for me, it strengthened my belief that the arc of women's history bends toward an inclusive narrative. As history practitioners, it is our responsibility to foster this progress, not just during major events such as the centennial, but also in our ongoing work.

As we interpret history for our visitors at museums and historic sites, we must present an accurate historical narrative and let each visitor engage with and accept or reject that history, on their own terms. It is important to note that not everyone will be able to reconcile issues of race and racism within the content as anything less than harmful. That said, organizations such as SBHM must do the difficult work of challenging the traditional narratives about women's suffrage that exclude issues of race and racism regardless of the public response. We must accept that their reaction may include an upwelling of disappointment and anger, resulting in disengagement from the content, and possibly from the organization as well.

2020: Commemorating the Centennial in Turbulent Times

Just as the political and cultural changes of the twentieth century greatly impacted the anniversaries of 1945, 1970, and 1995, the centennial was equally affected. In early 2020 as historic sites and museums prepared to kick off their centennial events and programs, the outbreak of COVID-19 created a dual health and economic crisis. On a national scale, the pandemic resulted in a staggering loss of life and shuttered businesses. For public history practitioners it also required a significant shift to virtual programming.[4] Amid the raging virus, the killings of George Floyd, Ahmaud Arbery, and Breonna Taylor sparked nationwide social justice protests and civil unrest. By late summer, the divisive presidential election cycle was underway and culminated in the celebrated but contested election of Kamala Harris as the first female, first Black, and first South Asian vice president of the United States along with President Joe Biden.[5] These national and global events had a significant impact on the tone, content, and level of public participation for the centennial.

To that end, many cultural institutions recognized that these developments allowed for critical discussions about race and racism. It also prompted practitioners to examine their role in contemporary social justice initiatives.[6] To illustrate one example, the American Alliance of Museums held their annual meeting virtually, which included a panel featuring museum leaders Lori Fogarty and Johnnetta B. Cole as well as secretary of the Smithsonian Lonnie G. Bunch III. The participants engaged in a robust dialogue around racial reckoning and how our museums and institutions should engage and even lead this vital work.[7]

Despite the dramatic social, economic, and political developments, both practitioners and scholars significantly contributed to the commemoration of the centennial. On the national level the major exhibitions at renowned institutions such as the National Portrait Gallery, Library of Congress, and National Archive, all in Washington, DC, exceeded expectations. The curators at each institution deftly presented the content that included a comprehensive narrative that highlighted Black, Indigenous, and people of color (BIPOC) who worked for women's enfranchisement, the expansion of voting rights, and women's equality.[8] Also the National Collaborative for Women's History Sites (NCWHS) expanded the National Votes for Women Trail (NVWT), which documents more than two thousand historic markers recognizing the women who worked for enfranchisement and political equality.[9] The database provides entries from every state, and a partnership with the William G. Pomeroy Foundation covered the cost of marker production and installation.[10] The online map provides many notable examples of enfranchisement efforts outside of urban centers and highlights suffragists who worked outside of national organizations. The NVWT

Figure 11.2.   Library of Congress "Shall Not Be Denied: Women Fight for the Vote" exhibit, taken June 4, 2019. Photo by author

is a valuable resource for practitioners who work in less populated areas and for smaller institutions that are looking for local resources.

Taken together, the major exhibitions in Washington, DC, and the newly documented historic content from NVWT will positively influence and advance our work as we expand the suffrage narrative. Even so, practitioners have more work ahead if we are to understand the overall impact of the 2020 centennial. As a field we will need to reflect and analyze the impact of the social, political, and cultural shifts as we continue to place women's equality and political activity within the larger arc of U.S. history.

Practical Strategies for Moving Forward

Given the decades of scholarship and resources available to us, it is without question that racism was omnipresent in late-nineteenth-century American society—whether it was acknowledged or not. As practitioners and educators, we will certainly continue to uncover issues of bias and racism within our historical narratives and at our institutions. Instead of pushing aside these difficult issues, we should push through them. Looking back at the case studies in the previous chapters, we see examples from practitioners who chose to reexamine the history of their organization in order to confront issues of bias and racism. Some were able to make great progress; however, others fell short of their own expectations. Nonetheless, I believe that there is as much to be learned from the less effective attempts as the successful ones. Taken together the case studies and previous chapters offer a path for practitioners to move forward in their work. The following is a concise review of several key strategies featured in the overall narrative.

1. Utilize Nontraditional Resources and Colleagues

As we learned from our colleagues Cindy Grisham, Rebecca Price, and Noelle Trent, we should question when our initial search results yield little to no information and then pivot to find other sources. Grisham recounts her lengthy search to discover the identity of Martha Stalker. During her research, Grisham encountered multiple barriers and ultimately relied on her law enforcement background to complete her search. In the Chick History case study, Rebecca Price shared her project "Protecting the Legacy," which documented African American women's political history in Tennessee before 1930. Her work, conducted in partnership with local communities, allowed the project to document and preserve the contributions and experiences of African American women. Noelle Trent reminds us to keep our implicit biases in check by beginning with the assumption that women were at the center of a historical narrative, instead of trying to fit them in to an existing male dominated narrative. Taken together, their collective work offers us the practical guidance to proactively seek out local partnerships, search for resources in nontraditional locations, and reject any narrative that assumes women did not contribute.

2. Avoid Defaulting to Binary Language

Acknowledging bias and systemic racism in historical narratives and within institutions is a complex undertaking. During my tenure as executive director of SBHM, I was unsuccessful in my attempt to address the problematic history of the NWP. Looking back, I recognize that our work stalled largely due to the difficulty of communicating the difference between racist actions by an individual versus the systemic racism that was part of the larger suffrage movement. Author and educator Robin DiAngelo cautions us to avoid applying binary labels that divide historic figures into categories of either "good" or "bad" people. In my experience, conversations that use this type of definitive language are actually counterproductive, and rarely result in a useful and productive dialogue. Instead we should begin the discussion by delving into the larger ramifications of systemic racism within the extensive historic narrative or institutional history.

3. Convene Open-Ended and Inclusive Conversations

Beginning conversations that reveal issues of bias and racism within historic narratives or institutions is complicated. However, trying to exert control over the dialogue is not the answer. A key factor is to ensure that the conversation is not limited to a small group of stakeholders. Productive conversations bring together participants from multiple communities, which allows for different perspectives. This expanded group is able to explore biases and systemic racism, ask new questions, and allow the participants to come away with a deeper understanding of the needs of both the organization and the community. Nonprofit professional Janedra Sykes, who specializes in racial equity, is a proponent of authentic and unscripted dialogue and encourages us to commit to investing as much time as needed to the process.

That said, beginning a narrative with a common level of understanding is critical to success. The Voting Rights Discussion Guide produced by the International Coalition of Sites of Conscience is a useful tool. The guide begins with a historical narrative around voting rights, which allows participants to set both their knowledge and expectations going forward. In the FWHM case study, Lori Osborne shows us that convening ongoing community conversations during the early and even developmental phase of the work is critical. This allows the public to become an early thought partners in the work, which increases the chance of overall success.

Final Thoughts

Given that the path to women's enfranchisement was both circuitous and fraught with divisions, it is therefore unsurprising that the legacy of suffrage is equally complicated. Even so, this new legacy is not a destination to arrive at; instead, it will be defined by the ongoing work at museums and historic sites across the country. This work must include an ongoing and comprehensive public dialogue on the full breadth of women's enfranchisement—one that includes an honest look at the systemic racism that is interwoven within the historic narrative. If we are successful, then our collective work will be seen as the new legacy of women's suffrage—one that lifts up the contributions and voices of all women, in communities of all sizes, and across the country.

Notes

1. For more information about Shirley Chisholm and Patsy Mink, see Debra Michals, "Shirley Chisholm," National Women's History Museum, 2015, www.womenshistory.org/education-resources/biographies/shirley-chisholm; and Kerri Lee Alexander, "Patsy Mink," National Women's History Museum, 2019, www.womenshistory.org/education-resources/biographies/patsy-mink.

2. Chitra Panjabi, "Becoming American," September 17, 2015, www.sewallbelmont.org/becoming-american (site deleted).

3. The White House, "Presidential Proclamation—Establishment of the Belmont-Paul Women's Equality National Monument," press release, April 12, 2016, https://obamawhitehouse.archives.gov/the-press-office/2016/04/12/presidential-proclamation-establishment-belmont-paul-womens-equality. For information on Equal Pay Day, see "Equal Pay Day Calendar," American Association of University Women, accessed February 1, 2021, www.aauw.org/resources/article/equal-pay-day-calendar. The Belmont-Paul Women's Equality National Monument was named for Alva Vanderbilt Belmont and Alice Stokes Paul.

4. Deborah Vankin, "How Hard Has COVID Hit American Museums? A New Survey Predicts a Grim Future," *Los Angeles Times*, November 11, 2020, www.latimes.com/entertainment-arts/story/2020-11-17/aam-american-alliance-museums-covid-survey. For more information, see the American Alliance for Museums website, "Maintaining Museum Excellence in the Time of COVID-19," American Alliance of Museums, January 13, 2021, www.aam-us.org/programs/about-museums/maintaining-museum-excellence-in-the-time-of-covid-19.

5. Brandon Tensley and Jasmine Wright, "Harris Bursts through Another Barrier, Becoming the First Female, First Black and First South Asian Vice President-Elect," *CNN*, November 7, 2020, www.cnn.com/2020/11/07/politics/kamala-harris-first-vice-president-female-black-south-asian/index.html.

6. Rachel Jones, "'I Want to Be Part of the Change': Why Thousands Are Demanding Racial Justice," *National Geographic*, June 7, 2020, www.nationalgeographic.com/history/2020/06/why-thousands-are-demanding-racial-justice/#close.

7. "Racism, Unrest, and the Role of the Museum Field," American Alliance of Museums, June 9, 2020, www.aam-us.org/2020/06/09/racism-unrest-and-the-role-of-the-museum-field.

8. The acronym *BIPOC* emerged in 2013. Sandra E. Garcia, "Where Did BIPOC Come From?" *New York Times*, June 17, 2020, www.nytimes.com/article/what-is-bipoc.html.

9. "National Votes for Women Trail," National Collaborative for Women's History Sites, accessed February 1, 2021, https://ncwhs.org/votes-for-women-trail.

10. "National Votes for Women Trail."

Appendix A
Timeline

THIS TIMELINE IS INCLUDED TO ENCOURAGE MUSEUM and historic site practitioners as they expand their interpretation of women's enfranchisement and voting rights. It begins in 1787 when the U.S. Constitution granted individual states the ability to determine voting qualifications, through 2018 when Deb Haaland and Sharice Davids became the first two Native American women elected to serve in the House of Representatives, and culminating in 2021 when Kamala Harris was sworn in as vice president and became the first woman, the first African American, and the first Asian American to hold the office. The timeline also includes the dates of key pieces of legislation and the pivotal work toward voting rights, civil rights, and women's equality.

1787	The U.S. Constitution grants states the ability to determine voting qualifications. Most states limit the franchise to only landowning White men.
1792	Mary Wollstonecraft pens *A Vindication of the Rights of Women*, calling for the equal education of men and women for the betterment of society.
1807	New Jersey limits voting to free White men only. It is the last state to prohibit women from voting.
1817	In an attempt to warn their nation to stop treaties with the federal government that included land cessions, thirteen Cherokee women send a petition to the Cherokee National Council. By the nineteenth century, Cherokee women lose their equitable standing with political decision-making; however, the petition uses their standings as mothers to argue their case.
1832	Free African American women organize the first entirely female abolitionist group, the Salem Female Anti-Slavery Society, in Salem, Massachusetts. That organization is followed in the next several years by numerous other female antislavery societies from northern states, with members primarily being free White women.
1837	The Anti-Slavery Convention of American Women meets in New York City. Several Black women attend and women's rights are a key issue.

1838	Sara Moore Grimké publishes the pamphlet "Letters on the Equality of the Sexes and the Condition of Women," calling for greater gender equity and especially for women to have the right to vote. She along with her sister, Angelina Grimké Weld, regularly lecture on abolition and women's rights.
1840	The World's Anti-Slavery Convention meets in London and determines that women, including Elizabeth Cady Stanton and Lucretia Mott, can observe but not participate in the proceedings.
1848	Lucretia Mott and her sister, Martha Coffin Wright, Elizabeth Cady Stanton, and Mary Ann M'Clintock hold the first women's rights convention in Seneca Falls, New York. Sixty-eight women and thirty-two men sign the Declaration of Sentiments, outlining the goals of the women's rights movement, including owning property, voting, and the full rights of citizenship. The women are inspired by the Haudenosaunee of New York.
1850	The first National Women's Rights Convention, organized by Lucy Stone, is held in Worcester, Massachusetts. Stone helps organize the American Woman Suffrage Association in 1869.
1851	Sojourner Truth delivers "I Am as Strong as Any Man" speech in Akron, Ohio. Born into slavery in New York in 1797, Truth denounces the name given to her as a slave, Isabella Baumfree, upon her emancipation and pursues her chosen vocation as an itinerant preacher. Starting in 1846, Truth lectures on abolitionism and becomes a powerful voice due to her history as a slave.
1865	The states ratify the Thirteenth Amendment abolishing slavery in the United States.
1866	The American Equal Rights Association is founded in Boston with the intent to secure equal rights and suffrage for all, regardless of race or sex.
1868	The states ratify the Fourteenth Amendment, defining citizenship and guaranteeing equal protection under the law.
1869	The Wyoming Territory legislature grants women the right to vote and hold public office.
	The suffrage movement splits into two factions over the Fifteenth Amendment. Anthony and Stanton refuse to support the Amendment and form the National Woman Suffrage Association (NWSA). The NWSA adopts a strategy focused on securing a federal constitutional amendment. Lucy Stone, Henry Blackwell, and Julia Ward Howe support the Fifteenth Amendment and form the American Woman Suffrage Association (AWSA). The AWSA focuses on a state-by-state campaign for suffrage.
1870	The states ratify the Fifteenth Amendment granting the right to vote to Black men. The NWSA, including Anthony and Stanton, refuse to support its ratification.
1871	Victoria Woodhull announces her candidacy for president of the United States. The Equal Rights Party nominates her, along with Frederick Douglass for vice president, in 1872.
	Abigail Scott Dunaway establishes *The New Northwest* in Portland, Oregon, which becomes a mouthpiece for social justice, including women's right to vote.
1872	Fifteen women, including Anthony, vote in Rochester, New York, as part of the NWSA strategy to use the Fourteenth Amendment to challenge laws prohibiting women voting. Anthony is arrested on November 18 and charged with illegally voting. Justice Ward Hunt convicts Anthony and sentences her to pay $100, which she never pays.
	Sojourner Truth is prevented from voting in Battle Creek, Michigan.

1874	Temperance advocates form the Woman's Christian Temperance Union (WCTU). Annie Wittenmyer is chosen as the first president.
1875	Congress passes the Page Act, banning Chinese women from immigrating to the United States.
	The U.S. Supreme Court unanimously rules in *Minor v. Happersett* that while Virginia Minor of St. Louis, Missouri, is a citizen, voting is not a right, but a privilege bestowed by the federal government, giving her no standing to sue the election official who prevented her from voting.
1878	Senator Aaron Augustus Sargent introduces the first women's suffrage amendment, drafted by Anthony and Stanton. Popularly called the Susan B. Anthony Amendment, the wording remains unchanged when it is finally passed in 1919.
1879	Frances Willard is elected president of the WCTU. She advocates women's suffrage as a means to social reform. The WCTU formerly endorses suffrage in 1881.
1882	Congress passes the Chinese Exclusion Act, preventing Chinese people who are not part of the merchant class from entering the United States.
1884	Lawyer Belva Lockwood accepts the nomination of the National Equal Rights party to run for president of the United States.
1885	Emma Goldman emigrates from Russia to New York and begins working in a garment factory in Rochester. An infamous anarchist, in addition to workers' rights advocate, Goldman fights for working-class women to have control over their reproductive selves.
1886	The Knights of Labor appoint the widow Leonora Barry as head of their Woman's Department. As an Irish-born garment worker, Barry pushes for the abolition of the Woman's Department on the grounds that women's membership in the union should hold no distinction due to their sex.
1889	Jane Addams and Ellen Gates Starr establish the Hull House in Chicago's Back of the Yards district. The settlement house becomes known for honoring the cultures of the immigrant families it serves, and providing workers with a place to hold union meetings and discuss political decisions. Settlement houses soon appear in major cities throughout the United States.
1890	The NWSA and the AWSA combine to form the National American Woman Suffrage Association (NAWSA). Stanton is the first president.
	The General Federation of Women's Clubs forms in New York at the calling of Jane Cunningham Croly. They do not formally endorse suffrage until 1914.
1893	Colorado grants women the right to vote.
	Hannah G. Solomon founds the National Council of Jewish Women in Chicago after Jewish women are excluded from meaningful contributions to the World's Fair. Its members promote the suffrage movement.
1894	Josephine St. Pierre Ruffin founds the Woman's Era Club in Boston. Both White and Black women join.
1895	Utah grants women the right to vote.
1896	Idaho grants women the right to vote.
	Black women found the National Association of Colored Women, a federation of Black women's clubs, with the motto "Lifting as We Climb." Ruffin organizes the founding meeting. Mary Church Terrell becomes the first president.

1900	Ruffin is prevented from representing the Woman's Era Club at the General Federation of Women's Club meeting.
	The International Ladies Garment Workers Union is founded by delegates representing unions in eastern cities and with members who were primarily Jewish immigrants.
1903	The Women's Trade Union League (WTUL) is founded at the American Federation of Labor convention. The WTUL organizes female labor, including a working-class suffrage movement committed to the vote and improving working conditions.
1904	The National Association of Colored Women incorporates as the National Association of Colored Women's Clubs.
1907	Congress passes the Expatriation Act, revoking American citizenship from American women who marry foreign men.
1908	Alpha Kappa Alpha sorority, the first Greek letter sorority for Black college women, is founded at Howard University by Ethel Hedgeman and fifteen other women. The sorority is chartered in 1913.
1909	The National Association for the Advancement of Colored People is founded following a riot in Springfield, Illinois. W. E. B. Du Bois, Ida B. Wells-Barnett, Terrell, and others attend the initial meeting to address racial justice called for by Mary White Ovington, Oswald Garrison Villard, William English Walling, and Dr. Henry Moscowitz.
1910	The state of Washington grants women the right to vote.
1911	California grants women the right to vote.
	(March 25) The Triangle Shirtwaist Factory catches on fire, killing 123 women and 23 men. The fire reinforces working-class women's view that they need the vote to protect themselves and secure better working conditions.
1912	Michigan, Kansas, Oregon, and Arizona grant women the right to vote.
1913	Former members of Alpha Kappa Alpha found Delta Sigma Theta at Howard University to create a sorority more focused on social issues, including suffrage. Delta Sigma Theta members march in the suffrage parade in Washington, DC.
	(March 3) Suffragists hold the Suffrage Procession in Washington, DC. The Congressional Committee organizes the event for the day before Woodrow Wilson's inauguration. More than eight thousand people participate, though White organizers segregate Black women to the back of the parade. Wells-Barnett and others refuse to march in the rear and join the Illinois unit in the middle of the procession.
	Alice Paul forms the Congressional Union for Woman Suffrage in addition to chairing the Congressional Committee of the NAWSA. The following year, the Congressional Union severs ties with the NAWSA due to Paul's militant approach.
	Illinois grants women the right to vote only in presidential elections.
	Wells-Barnett founds the Alpha Suffrage Club in Chicago. The club aims to organize and inform Black suffragists, increase political involvement, and elect Black officials.
1914	Montana and Nevada grant women the right to vote.
1915	The U.S. House of Representatives votes on a woman suffrage amendment for the first time. It fails 204 to 174.
	Nannie Helen Burroughs publishes "Black Women and Suffrage" in the August issue of *Crisis*.

1916	The Congressional Union forms the National Woman's Party in Chicago. The Congressional Union and National Woman's Party continue to coexist until 1917.
	Jeannette Rankin from Montana is the first woman elected to the U.S. House of Representatives.
1917	New York grants women the right to vote.
	Arkansas grants women the right to vote in primary, but not general, elections.
	Nebraska, North Dakota, Indiana, and Rhode Island grant women the right to partial suffrage.
	The Congressional Union and the National Woman's Party merge into one National Woman's Party under the leadership of Paul.
	In June, the NAACP organizes ten thousand African American men and women to silently march down New York City's Fifth Avenue to protest the riots in East St. Louis, Illinois.
1918	South Dakota, Oklahoma, and Michigan grant women the right to vote.
	Numerous suffragists are arrested for demonstrating in Lafayette Square in Washington, DC. The women are sentenced to the old District workhouse, where they go on hunger strikes.
1919	The U.S. House of Representatives and the U.S. Senate pass the Nineteenth Amendment and send it to the states for ratification.
1920	Zeta Phi Beta is founded at Howard University to promote causes of the Black community and social reform.
	Carrie Chapman Catt founds the League of Women's Voters at the NAWSA convention. Maud Wood Park is elected first president. The League encourages women to be politically engaged.
	(August 26) Secretary of State Bainbridge Colby signs the Nineteenth Amendment into law.
	Mary Morris Burnett Talbert is the first African American delegate appointed to the International Council of Women. A president of Buffalo, New York's, National Association of Colored Women from 1916 to 1920, Talbert also serves as the executive director of the NAACP's anti-lynching campaign.
1922	The Sigma Gamma Rho sorority is founded at Butler University in Indianapolis as a sorority for Black professional teachers. The sorority eventually expands to include undergraduate students.
	Congress passes the Cable Act, allowing women to retain their citizenship if married to a non-U.S. citizen eligible for naturalization.
1923	Paul drafts the Equal Rights Amendment (ERA). Senator Charles Curtis and Representative Daniel Anthony, both of Kansas, introduce the ERA in Congress.
1924	Congress passes the Indian Citizenship Act, granting national citizenship to all American Indians born in the United States. States continue to restrict American Indians' citizenship until 1962, when the last state, New Mexico, grants full citizenship.
1928	The Arizona Supreme Court rules in *Porter v. Hall* that Native Americans are ineligible to vote in Arizona, as they are wards of the federal government. The Arizona Supreme Court reverses its ruling in *Harrison v. Laveen* in 1948.

1929	The League of United Latin American Citizens (LULAC) forms to unite organizations working for the civil rights of Mexican Americans. Ben Garza leads the effort, bringing together delegates from numerous organizations across Texas, including the Order of the Sons of America, the Knights of America, and the League of Latin American Citizens. In 1934, Ester Machuca forms Ladies LULAC Council #9. In 1938, Machuca becomes the first Ladies Organizer General.
1935	Mary McLeod Bethune founds the National Council of Negro Women in Washington, DC, as an umbrella organization to improve the lives of Black women.
1937	Congress repeals Section 213 of the Legislative Appropriations Act (Economy Act) of 1932, which required married persons to be fired before unmarried persons, if their spouse were also a federal employee. The NWP works for its repeal, but is unsuccessful in securing a provision to rehire fired workers, most of whom were women.
1943	Congress repeals the Chinese Exclusion Act. The bill is a compromise in that it allows Chinese immigrants to enter the United States, but it creates a quota limiting visas for Chinese immigrants to 105 per year based on race, rather than citizenship or national origin.
1945	The NWP and the World Woman's Party (WWP) successfully lobby the United Nations to include gender equality in its charter. The NWP and WWP also successfully persuade the UN to include equality provisions in its Universal Declaration of Human Rights in 1948.
1946	The Women's Political Caucus (WPC) is established in Montgomery, Alabama, to advocate for voting rights and desegregation. Led by educator JoAnn Gipson Robinson, most members are African American professional women. The group is most known for their organization in 1955 of the Montgomery bus boycotts.
1947	Region 1-A's Women's Committee of the United Auto Workers is established in Detroit, Michigan, to advocate for workers' rights.
1952	Congress passes the McCarran-Walter Act, allowing Asian immigrants to enter the United States and Asian Americans to obtain citizenship. The act continues to base immigration on quotas, and uses race, rather than citizenship, as the basis for quotas for Asian immigrants.
1953	The Daughters of Bilitis, the first lesbian rights organization, forms in San Francisco.
1960	The Student Nonviolent Coordinating Committee (SNCC) organizes sit-ins at lunch counters throughout the south. Fisk University student Diane Nash begins her civil rights activism with the sit-ins, and one year later becomes a leader in SNCC's Freedom Rides.
1961	The Kennedy Administration creates the Commission on the Status of Women. The Equal Pay Act results in 1963.
1962	Dolores Huerta and César Chavez organize the United Farm Workers. Huerta serves as a major advocate for the rights of Latinas into the twenty-first century.
1964	(January 23) The states ratify the Twenty-Fourth Amendment. It prohibits the use of poll taxes as a condition of voting.
	Congress passes the Civil Rights Act, with the inclusion of Title VII, prohibiting employment discrimination based on race, color, religion, sex, and national origin. The NWP campaigns for Title VII's inclusion.
	The Mississippi Freedom Democratic Party is established as a challenge to the all-White Mississippi Democratic Party. The party argues to be seated at the Democratic National Convention in Atlantic City. Leaders include Fannie Lou Hamer and Ella Baker, who are active organizers in SNCC.

1964	Freedom Summer brings thousands of volunteers, most of whom are White college and university students, to southern states to assist African American groups (organized as the Council of Federated Organizations) register African Americans to vote.
1965	Congress passes the Voting Rights Act, enforcing voting rights for racial minorities and prohibiting racial discrimination in voting. The act requires preclearance before changing election laws in areas with discriminatory voting requirements.
1966	The National Organization for Women is founded.
	The National Welfare Rights Organization is founded.
1969	Shirley Chisholm becomes the first African American woman to be elected to Congress. She serves six terms. In 1971, she is a founding member of both the Congressional Black Caucus and the National Women's Political Caucus.
1971	(July 1) The Twenty-Sixth Amendment is ratified, lowering the voting age to 18.
	The U.S. House of Representatives passes the ERA.
	Anna Nieto-Gomez and other Chicana women at California State University–Long Beach found Hijas de Cuauhtémoc (Daughters of Cuauhtémoc) to advocate for the rights of Mexican American women.
1972	The U.S. Senate passes the ERA, sending the amendment to the states for ratification. The amendment has yet to be ratified.
	Chisholm becomes the first African American to run for president, as well as the first Democratic woman to run for president, doing so against the segregationist George Wallace.
1973	The National Black Feminist Organization is formed during the summer in New York City to combat both the racism and sexism Black women face. The group's members include Florynce Kennedy, Margo Jefferson, Faith Ringgold, Michelle Wallace, and Doris Wright.
1974	Over two hundred women activists from thirty nations establish Women of All Red Nations (WARN) out of concern over the acknowledgment that the Indian Health Service has been sterilizing American Indian women without their consent.
1975	Congress extends the Voting Rights Act for seven years. It also amends the act to include bilingual election requirements, expanding the vote to previously excluded groups including Hispanics, Native Americans, and Asian Americans.
1977	A group of African American feminists, many of whom identify as lesbian, create the Combahee River Collective and author "A Black Feminist Statement," emphasizing that the oppression experienced by women of color results from the intersections of race, class, and sex.
	The National Women's Conference is held in Houston, Texas. Two thousand delegates from fifty states and six territories participate in voting on over twenty planks while an additional fifteen thousand to twenty thousand women attend as observers. The conference is authorized by public law and supported with federal funds. Dignitaries such as former and current first ladies participate alongside former and current political representatives such as U.S. representative Barbara Jordan.
1993	The National Voter Registration Act (NVRA) advances voting rights by requiring states to simplify voter registration processes. Referred to as the "Motor Voter Law," it creates a mail-in form that allows citizens to register to vote when obtaining services at government agencies such as the Department of Motor Vehicles.

2009	First enacted in 1986, the Uniformed and Overseas Citizen Absentee Voter Act (UOCAVA) protects the right to vote in federal elections for members of the military (and families) serving overseas and U.S. citizens who reside overseas. It was expanded in 2009 as the Military and Overseas Voter Empowerment (MOVE) Act and requires states to transmit validly requested absentee ballots to those voters no later than forty-five days before a federal election.
2013	The Supreme Court finds part of the Voting Rights Act unconstitutional in *Shelby County v. Holder*. It rules the formula used to determine areas necessitating preclearance are outdated, allowing these areas to change voting requirements without federal oversight.
2017	(January 21) The "Women's March on Washington" takes place to protest the inauguration of President Donald Trump. While the main march takes place in Washington, DC, protestors march across the country and around the world. It is widely believed to be the largest single-day demonstration in the country.
2018	Deb Haaland, a member of the Laguna Pueblo, is elected to represent New Mexico in the House of Representatives. Sharice Davids, a member of the Ho-Chunk Nation, is elected to represent Kansas. These two women are the first Native American women elected to Congress.
2021	(January 21) Kamala Harris is sworn in as vice president of the United States by Supreme Court Justice Sonia Sotomayor. Harris becomes the first woman, the first African American, and the first Asian American to hold the office.

Appendix B
Resources

Autry, La Tanya S., ed. "Social Justice & Museums Resource List." Crowdsourced Document. https://artstuffmatters.wordpress.com/social-justice-museums-resources.

In 2015, cultural organizer La Tanya S. Autry started the "Social Justice & Museums Resource List," a crowd-sourced bibliography hosted on Google Docs that explored museum practices, challenges, and experiences through an intersectional lens. Autry encouraged museum professionals, students, educators, and activists to utilize the bibliography in research and to contribute additional sources to the list. The list included over four hundred essays, reports, exhibitions, videos, and programs, covering themes such as "Activism in Museums," "Race: Understanding the Construct," "Diversity, Inclusion, Equity," and "Decolonization." This robust list indicated museums' changing role in society and the increasing expectation that museums should have a viewpoint in cultural and political conversations. Though the document has since been deleted, Autry discusses the list on her blog, Artstuffmatters.

Benson, Virginia R. *American Women's History Journey.* https://americanwomenshistoryjourney.com.

In 2018, historian Virginia Bensen launched *American Women's History Journey: An Interactive E-Zine & Podcast.* The e-zine website features articles by Bensen, blog posts highlighting women's history resources and content from various organizations, book recommendations, and the *American Women's History Journey Podcast.* As of this writing, the first introductory episode of the podcast is posted on the website. Future episodes will feature authors of American women's history books. Scholars can submit articles to be posted on the website or request to be a guest on the podcast.

Gaskell, Tamara, ed. "19th Amendment and Women's Access to the Vote Across America." National Parks Service, April 5, 2019. www.nps.gov/subjects/womenshistory/women-s-access-to-the-vote.htm.

This series of NPS essays documents the evolution of woman suffrage from its roots in the reform movements of the 1830s to its militant conclusion and ratification of the Nineteenth

Amendment in 1920. The essays examine the regional differences among suffragists, as well as the varying tactics of key figures. Some of these tactics included using the press and images to garner support, international cooperation, and partnering with other reform groups such as temperance advocates, the labor movement, socialists, and progressives. These scholars pay particular attention to the split among suffragists over the Fifteenth Amendment and the state-by-state versus federal approach to granting the vote. The essays also highlight the contributions and organizations of Black suffragists, despite their exclusion from national organizations. Though the Nineteenth Amendment was ratified in 1920, the final essay describes its limitations and the women who remained disenfranchised but continued to work for suffrage following its passage.

Green, Amara. "Black Feminism Introductory Research Guide." New York Public Library. https://libguides.nypl.org/blackfeminism.

This digital guide, compiled by scholar Amara Green and published in 2018, highlights the works of black women found within the collections of the New York Public Library's Schomburg Center for Research in Black Culture. This resource provides researchers with a free, introductory guide to the essential works of black feminism, featuring prominent figures such as Alice Walker, Zora Neale Hurston, Audre Lorde, Angela Davis, and more. Materials listed in the guide include books, film, and audio recordings primarily found in the Schomburg Center's collection, but also from throughout the New York Public Library. Researchers can search the guide by author or key terms, or browse by categories such as "Literature," "Manuscripts and Archives," "Art and Artists," and others.

Mauer, Elizabeth L., Jeanette Patrick, Liesle M. Britto, and Henry Miller. *Where Are the Women? A Report on the Status of Women in the United States Social Studies Standards.* National Women's History Museum, 2018. www.womenshistory.org/sites/default/files/museum-assets/document/2018-02/NWHM_Status-of-Women-in-State-Social-Studies-Standards_2-27-18.pdf.

In this report, the National Women's History Museum (NWHM) examines the representation of women's history in state social studies curriculum standards. The NWHM project team reviewed standards for all fifty states and the District of Columbia, and added each standard that refers to a woman or women-related topic into a database. From their analysis of the data, the team concluded that women are underrepresented in most state history standards. The National Women's History Museum is using the findings of the report to create women's history materials that will be most beneficial to teachers in the classroom. The report is free to download from the NWHM website, and provides a useful resource to find data on the state of women's history in classrooms across the country.

"Remarkable Legacies of American Women." National Park Service. www.nps.gov/subjects/womenshistory/index.htm.

This "Women's History" section of the National Park Service (NPS) website is produced by the NPS and NPS partners, including the National Conference of State Historic Preservation Officers. This portal provides information about the fight for women's suffrage, a breakdown of each state's role in the movement and the passage of the Nineteenth Amendment, a chance to explore women's history by subject, and an introduction to women's history in the United States that emphasizes the diversity of women's experiences. This site provides a cursory overview of women's history that should be helpful in introducing the subject to new audiences. It also includes free education materials and tools for students, teachers, parents, and public historians, and it lists national parks to visit that focus on women's history, such as the Belmont-Paul Women's Equality National Monument, the Clara Barton National Historic Site, Harriet Tubman National Historic Park, and more.

Smith, Christen A. *Cite Black Women*. www.citeblackwomencollective.org.

Founded in 2017, Cite Black Women is a campaign using slogan t-shirts, social media, web content, and a podcast to increase awareness and acknowledgment of the intellectual contributions of Black women, whose works are often undercited and underappreciated. On social media, the campaign encourages followers to quote works by Black women using the hashtags #CiteBlackWomen and #CiteBlackWomenSunday as a method of crowdsourcing information about Black women's scholarly and artistic works. Cite Black Women uses its various media to provide free, accessible platforms to discover works by Black women and to engage in conversation about the politics behind citation practices.

"Suffrage in America: The 15th and 19th Amendments." National Park Service. www.nps.gov/subjects/womenshistory/15th-and-19th-amendments.htm.

On this page of the "Women's History" section of their website, the National Park Service provides a brief background on the history of voting rights in the United States, and shares links to NPS articles that focus on different eras in the expansion of the franchise. These articles provide an overview of the fight for voting rights in the United States, from the country's founding, through the women's suffrage and Civil Rights movements, to today. Each article contains one to three discussion questions, making this resource a helpful tool for the classroom or women's history workshops.

"Tribal Nations and the United States: An Introduction." National Congress of American Indians. www.ncai.org/resources/ncai_publications/tribal-nations-and-the-united-states-an-introduction.

The National Congress of American Indians' "Tribal Nations and the United States: An Introduction" provides an overview of the political structure and demography of tribal nations within the United States. Beginning first with a history of tribal nations' influence on American democracy, the guide identifies key historical periods characterizing the relationship between tribal nations and the federal government. It then outlines different approaches to tribal governance. Most significantly, the document explains tribal nations' status as "nations within a nation" and the responsibilities of recognized tribal nations, state, and federal governments to each other. It also frames the rights of individuals within tribal nations, as citizens of both their own tribe and the United States. The guide ends with a summary of challenges tribal nations face, including poverty and unemployment, and the measures they are currently taking to address these issues, such as gaming. Using helpful infographics, the publication serves as a useful introduction to appropriate terminology, basic history, and the relationship between tribal nations and the United States.

Women Also Know History. https://womenalsoknowhistory.com.

With its website and social media campaign, Women Also Know History fosters an online community elevating the work and expertise of women historians. On the website, women historians can build their own profiles, describing their backgrounds, areas of expertise, and published works, identifying relevant searchable key terms, and listing their contact information. Researchers or members of the media who are looking for sources can search key terms to find relevant historians, or can browse lists of historians by areas of expertise. This free, user-friendly website is a valuable resource that is elevating the work of women historians. Women Also Know History encourages scholars to spread the word by posting to social media with their hashtag and referring colleagues and media to the website.

"Women's History." Alexander Street Press. https://alexanderstreet.com/discipline/womens-history.
    Alexander Street Press's digital collection, "Women's History," provides access to multiple databases with hundreds of primary sources regarding women's history. Organized into several collections, such as "Women and Social Movements in the United States, 1600 to 2000" and "Women and Social Movements International," subscribers can access newsreels, videos, digitized archival documents, a biographical dictionary, oral histories, and scholarly essays analyzing the collection. In addition to sources from well-known figures such as Elizabeth Cady Stanton, the collection highlights resources unavailable in other collections from lesser-known historical figures. Accessing the database does require a subscription, although Alexander Street offers a thirty-day free trial.

Women's Suffrage Centennial Commission. Archived December 2020. www.womensvote100.org.
    In 2017, Congress created the Women's Suffrage Centennial Commission to oversee the 100th anniversary of the passage of the Nineteenth Amendment. The commission, chaired by Susan Combs, coordinated nationwide efforts between governments and private entities to celebrate the centennial throughout 2020. The website includes information regarding programs, art displays, talks, activities for kids, and articles written by historians exploring the history of women's suffrage. The site also includes an archive of media coverage regarding anniversary events, and the commission's final report, documenting federal commemorations, the impact of centennial programs, and a list of events. Even though the commission disbanded on December 18, 2020, the website was archived, preserving the commission's work.

Women's Vote Centennial Initiative. www.2020centennial.org.
    The 2020 Women's Vote Centennial Initiative (WVCI) is an information-sharing collaborative, created to promote the 100th anniversary of the Nineteenth Amendment and American women winning the constitutional right to vote. Founded in 2015, WVCI brings together representatives of national institutions, grassroots groups, and scholars to raise the visibility and increase the impact of this historic anniversary. The mission is to encourage efforts to commemorate the centennial of the Nineteenth Amendment across the country, educate the public on the legal and social advances resulting from the amendment, acknowledge the inadequacies of the movement and the amendment's implementation, and stimulate dialogue concerning the ongoing fight for equal rights. The website serves as a central organizing and information-sharing clearinghouse on the broad range of programs, exhibits, artistic works, and governmental and grassroots activities in states and localities around the country.

"Wyoming: Home of the Women's Vote." Wyoming Office of Tourism. Accessed August 5, 2019. www.travelwyoming.com/wyoming-womens-suffrage.

Wyoming was the first state to give women the right to vote, decades before passage of the Nineteenth Amendment. To commemorate the state's 150th anniversary of women's suffrage, the Wyoming Office of Tourism has declared 2019 the "Year of Wyoming Women." The campaign will run through 2020, encouraging tourists to visit historic sites and attend events in Wyoming related to women's history, planning retreats in the state geared toward women, and celebrating Wyoming women today by asking social media users to share their own stories using the hashtag #ThatsWYWomen.

Appendix C

AASLH Nineteenth Amendment Centennial Value Statement

T HE AASLH NINETEENTH AMENDMENT VALUE STATEMENT (Value Statement) offers guiding principles and starting points to serve as best practices and offer encouragement to AASLH members and the field for ways to interpret the centennial anniversary of the ratification of the Nineteenth Amendment.

AASLH 19th Amendment Centennial Value Statement

"The right of citizens of the United States to vote shall not be denied or abridged by the United States or by any State on account of sex."

ABOUT

The AASLH 19th Amendment Value Statement (Value Statement) offers Guiding Principles and Starting Points to serve as best practices and offer encouragement to AASLH members and the field for ways to interpret the Centennial Anniversary of the Ratification of the 19th Amendment.

AASLH serves a diverse audience. As such there are members whose mission it is to interpret the Civil Rights movement and institutions dedicated to highlighting the life and work of women, who will be able to address an extensive range of themes and perhaps even comment on public policy issues. There are also organizations on the other end of the spectrum, such as small museums, those not named for a woman, or those who fall outside of the time period who will not have as much leeway in their exhibits and programmatic offerings. As such, this Value Statement contains a range of methodologies to serve a diverse membership and to provide value to a variety of historic sites, museums, archives, and libraries.

This Value Statement is not meant to offer a step-by-step framework or model. This document is meant to offer guidance and suggestions that organizations can use to develop programming.

More than anything, this Value Statement is intended to inspire and advocate for new and innovative methods for interpretation, ones that can be shared, improved upon, and disseminated to the field.

VALUE STATEMENT

In 2020, the nation will mark the 100th Anniversary of the Ratification of the 19th Amendment. Women and men of all races, ethnicities, and identities fought for—and against—women's right to vote. It was a national movement carried out on the local level by tens of thousands of people across the country. It is one part a story about women's rights, but it is also equal parts an American story of race, class, citizenship, gender, immigration, political identity, and values, and the intersections where those meet in America's collective narrative and history.

The history of 19th Amendment is a complex narrative that encompasses multiple perspectives and points in time. It can be found in the days of the nation's founding and with the inspiration of Native American women on early feminist thought. It can be found in the racial schisms between universal suffrage and African American male suffrage following the Civil War. It can be found in local women's clubs and churches where women gathered in spaces that offered them leadership opportunities. And it can be found in its influence on historic events that came after it including voting rights, civil rights, and women's rights. It is a testament to, and a product of, America's founding ideals: the never-ending, quest for life, liberty, and the pursuit of happiness,

Figure C.1. AASLH 19th Amendment Centennial Value Statement, 2019.

and how our country adapts with each generation to address, define, and meet those inalienable rights.

The 100th Anniversary of the Ratification of the 19th Amendment presents an opportunity to expand the narrative of woman suffrage; challenge preconceptions and definitions about history; and engage with the proud, conflicted, and complex realities of our shared history.

GUIDING PRINCIPLES

Woman Suffrage vs. the Realities of the 19th Amendment

The quest for universal enfranchisement and increased rights for women expands beyond a series of campaigns, a geographic region, or a single economic class or political identity. Quite simply it was as diverse and varied as the American population. The final version of the 19th Amendment to the US Constitution was far more limited in scope and reach than the various campaigns had intended. Making comparisons between the fullness of women's demands, and the brevity of the 19th Amendment reveals a gap in our historic narrative and provides us the opportunity to delve into and share a myriad of unique and nuanced stories with visitors and provide new ways to connect to this historic content.

Acknowledging Divisions and Historical Reality

The need to acknowledge in authentic ways the racial, economic, religious, and political divisions of the suffrage movement is critical to our understanding of this narrative of American history. To delve in to the total arc of the woman suffrage movement we must include the complexities of generations of women and a political climate that spans the Early Republic to the Civil War and from Reconstruction to the Progressive Era and beyond. While discussing racial, economic, religious, and political intolerance is complicated, when done in an open and transparent manner, it can result in a more powerful experience and deeper understanding for the visitor, practitioner, and stakeholder.

Elevating Multiple Perspectives

The history of woman suffrage is nuanced, complex, diverse, and often includes conflicting storylines—depending on the author or timeframe. The experiences and histories of the thousands of women who fought for suffrage on the regional, state, and local levels are equally as important as the work of the national suffrage leaders. The different perspectives and reasons people fought for or against suffrage should be considered and presented in interpretation. Accordingly, AASLH members should continue to examine their interpretation process and ask, "Who is not included in our commemoration programming?" This will allow us to achieve an inclusive, diverse, and comprehensive commemoration of the 19th Amendment.

Recognizing Today's Intersectional Audience

Figure C.2.   AASLH 19th Amendment Centennial Value Statement, 2019.

The upcoming Centennial of the 19th Amendment offers exciting opportunities and dynamic challenges for viewing the past. It invites important questions about how we interpret historic events and how to connect those events with modern audiences. Much of today's audience views the past through the lens of the great civil and social justice movements of the late 1900s. Visitors expect exhibits to reflect the understandings of these movements in their historical interpretation. To create context for today's 21st Century, intersectional audience, interpretation should highlight the work of all the women who worked for suffrage, and at the same time, recognize the limitations and imperfections of the movement, and by extension, the American democratic process, and individual Americans.

Expanding Time and Place

The 19th Amendment's passage is a culmination of diverse and complex events and experiences that unfolded years, decades, even centuries before 1920. Sites and practitioners that interpret earlier periods of American history have the opportunity to share the lives and experiences of all the women associated with the site, and explore ways those particular conditions created a cumulative effect on views of women's roles, participation, and rights in American society. Organizations that offer historic content after 1920 have the opportunity to examine the ways and degrees in which those conditions and experiences changed, were successful, or were unsuccessful.

Preserving New Histories

There is still a critical lack of primary sources and histories about women available for interpretation and public programming. As a field and individual practitioners of history we can use the Centennial of the 19th Amendment as a chance to collect and document previously untold histories as part of commemoration events. Leave time for the exploration of unprocessed collections, or reach out to your community for help in finding documentation that may still reside in private hands. Concerted efforts to work with local communities to find and preserve these important histories, through physical documentation and oral histories, will expand our understanding of the time period and serve our communities well in to the future.

Looking Beyond the Iconic Story

The Centennial provides an entry-point into expanding the arc of the suffrage story by taking a fresh look at the past. Particularly for sites named for women, or who have suffrage collections, challenge your interpretation by using new material and primary sources. Go beyond your most recognized suffrage objects and dig into your collection and community to seek a different story to tell. Do not be afraid to give a higher priority, or start with, a lesser-known story from your collection or community.

Figure C.3.   AASLH 19th Amendment Centennial Value Statement, 2019.

STARTING POINTS

The following is a preliminary list of broad questions to consider that can aid with developing programming. By considering these as starting points for interpretation, and applying diverse, inclusive, and intersectional approaches, they offer a chance to reframe, broaden, and create a more authentic interpretation. Organizations should thoroughly consult their mission, audience, and community for themes and areas to address not included here. **This list should not be considered final by any definition.**

1. How did women build up their political power before 1920?
2. How did clubs, churches, and academic centers serve as sources of strength and places for African American women to express political and civic agendas?
3. How did the work of women writers in publications, journals, and the press advance civic and community issues?
4. What effect did the Civil War and WWI have on women and the movement?
5. What were the connections between the Abolition and Temperance movements?
6. How did society's views on race, gender roles, and idealized womanhood affect the "Public Face" of Woman Suffrage?
7. How did different regions of the country address woman's suffrage? What comparisons can be made between different regions, such as African American communities in Chicago versus the South; or progressive areas in the West versus elite communities in the Northeast?
8. How were the Suffrage Movement and women's community causes funded? Where did women find the money, from black-owned community businesses to wealthy patrons, etc.?
9. How did gender identity, sexual orientation, and women who challenged gender norms of the time period shape and advance the movement?
10. How did the suffrage campaign play out in the media, through editorials, cartoons, magazine, posters, post cards, etc.?
11. Who were the women and men suffrage leaders in your city, county, state?
12. Who were the women and men opposed to extending voting rights to women, and why, particularly across issues of race, ethnicity, and gender?
13. How did your city or state contribute to the struggle for Woman Suffrage? Were they supportive of local suffrage (voting on issues of schools and family), state suffrage, or enfranchisement at the federal level?
14. How did religious intolerance impact the campaigns for suffrage? Were members of some faith-based groups viewed differently, such as Catholics, Protestants, the Church of Jesus Christ of Latter-Day Saints (LDS) in the western states, Quaker Communities in the east, Jewish Communities, etc.?
15. How did citizenship status impact the voting rights of Mexican Americans, Native Americans, and Chinese immigrants in the western states?
16. How did women influence 20th century politics as candidates, public officials, advisors, and community leaders?
17. How did tactics such as literacy tests, poll taxes, and racial terror continue to repress votes, particularly for African Americans?

Figure C.4.   AASLH 19th Amendment Centennial Value Statement, 2019.

18. What are connections between the 19th Amendment and the Civil Rights Movements?
19. What are ways the 19th Amendment, and the politicizing of women's issues, have affected women's relationship with each other?
20. After the 19th Amendment, how did women stay involved in politics, activism, and public life? How did their roles change, or not change, in public life and leadership?
21. How is the history of the vote connected to contemporary movements for women's rights and women's political representation?
22. How has the definition of citizenship changed over time? How can the 19th Amendment offer a larger reflection on the narrative of American citizenship, the incremental nature of American citizenship, and how Americans have successfully and unsuccessfully fought for citizenship and rights?
23. If the 19th Amendment addresses one form of voter disenfranchisement, what are ways that political disenfranchisement exists today, and why?
24. What lessons can today's society learn from this political campaign?

The AASLH Women's History Affinity Group would like to thank everyone who participated in the 2018 Online Call for Comments and the AASLH Kansas City Annual Conference Roundtable for their thoughtful and candid feedback. Copyright 2019.

Figure C.5.   AASLH 19th Amendment Centennial Value Statement, 2019.

Bibliography

Adams, Katherine H., and Michael L. Keene. *Alice Paul and the American Suffrage Campaign*. Urbana: University of Illinois Press, 2008.

Balgooy, Max van, ed. *Interpreting African American History and Culture at Museums and Historic Sites*. Interpreting History. Lanham, MD: Rowman & Littlefield, 2015.

Berenson, Barbara F. *Massachusetts in the Woman Suffrage Movement: Revolutionary Reformers*. American Heritage. Charleston, SC: History Press, 2018.

Berry, Daina Ramey, and Kali Nicole Gross. *A Black Women's History of the United States*. Boston: Beacon Press, 2020.

Blair, Karen J. *The Clubwoman as Feminist: True Womanhood Redefined, 1868–1914*. New York: Holmes and Meier, 1980.

Blight, David. *Race and Reunion: The Civil War in American Memory*. Cambridge, MA: Harvard University Press, 2002.

Boylan, Anne M. *Women's Rights in the United States: A History in Documents*. Pages from History. New York: Oxford University Press, 2016.

Bruggeman, Seth C., ed. *Commemoration: The American Association for State and Local History Guide*. Lanham, MD: Rowman & Littlefield, 2017.

Bundles, A'Lelia Perry. *On Her Own Ground: The Life and Times of Madam C.J. Walker*. New York: Scribner, 2002.

Cahill, Bernadette. *Alice Paul, the National Woman's Party and the Vote: The First Civil Rights Struggle of the 20th Century*. Jefferson, NC: McFarland, 2015.

Cahill, Cathleen D. *Recasting the Vote: How Women of Color Transformed the Suffrage Movement*. Chapel Hill: University of North Carolina Press, 2020.

Church, Lila Teresa. "Documenting Local African American Community History: Some Guidelines for Consideration." In *Interpreting African American History and Culture at Museums and Historic Sites*, edited by Max van Balgooy, 61–74. Lanham, MD: Rowman & Littlefield, 2015.

Clift, Eleanor. *Founding Sisters and the Nineteenth Amendment*. Turning Points in American History. Hoboken, NJ: Wiley, 2003.

Coates, Ta-Nehisi. *Between the World and Me*. New York: Spiegel and Grau, 2015.

Cole, Johnnetta B., and Beverly Guy-Sheftall. *Gender Talk: The Struggle for Women's Equality in African American Communities*. New York: Ballantine Books, 2003.

Cordery, Stacy A. *Juliette Gordon Low: The Remarkable Founder of the Girl Scouts*. New York: Viking, 2012.

DiAngelo, Robin J. *White Fragility: Why It's So Hard for White People to Talk about Racism*. Boston: Beacon Press, 2018.

DuBois, Ellen Carol. *Feminism and Suffrage: The Emergence of an Independent Women's Movement in America, 1848–1869*. Ithaca, NY: Cornell University Press, 1978.

———. *Harriot Stanton Blatch and the Winning of Woman Suffrage*. New Haven, CT: Yale University Press, 1997.

———. *Suffrage: Women's Long Battle for the Vote*. New York: Simon and Schuster, 2020.

DuBois, Ellen Carol, and Vicki Ruíz, eds. *Unequal Sisters: A Multicultural Reader in U.S. Women's History*. New York: Routledge, 1990.

Dudden, Faye E. *Fighting Chance: The Struggle over Woman Suffrage and Black Suffrage in Reconstruction America*. New York: Oxford University Press, 2011.

Feimster, Crystal. *Southern Horrors: Women and the Politics of Rape and Lynching*. Cambridge, MA: Harvard University Press, 2011.

Ferentinos, Susan. *Interpreting LGBT History at Museums and Historic Sites*. Lanham, MD: Rowman & Littlefield, 2015.

Florey, Kenneth. *Women's Suffrage Memorabilia: An Illustrated Historical Study*. Jefferson, NC: McFarland, 2013.

Ford, Linda. *Iron-Jawed Angels: The Suffrage Militancy of the National Woman's Party, 1912–1920*. Lanham, MD: University Press of America, 1991.

Fox, Emma A., ed. *General Federation of Women's Clubs: Sixth Biennial Convention: Official Proceedings*. Detroit: John Bornman and Son, 1902.

Freeman, Jo. "Political Organization in the Feminist Movement." *Acta Sociologica* 18, no. 2–3 (1975): 222–44.

Giddings, Paula. *Ida: A Sword among Lions; Ida B. Wells and the Campaign against Lynching*. New York: Amistad, 2009.

———. *In Search of Sisterhood: Delta Sigma Theta and the Challenge of the Black Sorority Movement*. New York: Amistad, 1988.

———. *When and Where I Enter: The Impact of Black Women on Race and Sex in America*. New York: W. Morrow, 1996.

Gilmore, Glenda Elizabeth. *Gender and Jim Crow: Women and the Politics of White Supremacy in North Carolina, 1896–1920*. Chapel Hill: University of North Carolina Press, 1996.

Ginzberg, Lori D. *Elizabeth Cady Stanton: An American Life*. New York: Hill and Wang, 2009.

Gordon, Ann Dexter, and Bettye Collier-Thomas, eds. *African American Women and the Vote, 1837–1965*. Amherst: University of Massachusetts Press, 1997.

Green, Elna C. *Southern Strategies: Southern Women and the Woman Suffrage Question*. Chapel Hill: University of North Carolina Press, 1997.

Hendricks, Wanda A. *Fannie Barrier Williams: Crossing the Borders of Region and Race*. Urbana: University of Illinois Press, 2014.

Hernández, Daisy, and Bushra Rehman, eds. *Colonize This! Young Women of Color on Today's Feminism*. Emeryville, CA: Seal Press, 2002.

Houde, Mary Jean. *Reaching out: A Story of the General Federation of Women's Clubs*. Chicago: Mobium Press, 1989.

Jeffries, Hasan Kwame. *Understanding and Teaching the Civil Rights Movement*. Madison: University of Wisconsin Press, 2019.

Johnson, Barry. "Polarity Management." *Executive Development* 6, no. 2 (May 1993). doi:10.1108/EUM0000000003846.

Johnson, Joan Marie. "Following the Money: Wealthy Women, Feminism, and the American Suffrage Movement." *Journal of Women's History* 27, no. 4 (Winter 2015): 62–87. doi:10.1353/jowh.2015.0038.

———. *Funding Feminism: Monied Women, Philanthropy, and the Women's Movement, 1870–1967.* Gender and American Culture. Chapel Hill: University of North Carolina Press, 2017.

Jones, Martha S. *Vanguard: How Black Women Broke Barriers, Won the Vote, and Insisted on Equality for All.* New York: Basic Books, 2020.

Joyner, Brian D. *African Reflections on the American Landscape.* Washington, DC: U.S. Department of the Interior, National Park Service, National Center for Cultural Resources, Office of Diversity and Special Projects, 2003. www.nps.gov/heritageinitiatives/pubs/Africanisms.pdf

Kaba, Mariame, and Essence McDowell. *Lifting as They Climbed: Mapping a History of Black Women on Chicago's South Side, a Self-Guided Tour.* Chicago: Chicago Black Women Tour, 2018.

Lemak, Jennifer A., and Ashley Hopkins-Benton. *Votes for Women: Celebrating New York's Suffrage Centennial.* Excelsior Editions. Albany: State University of New York Press, 2017.

Materson, Lisa G. *For the Freedom of Her Race: Black Women and Electoral Politics in Illinois, 1877–1932.* Chapel Hill: University of North Carolina Press, 2009.

McClaurin, Irma, ed. *Black Feminist Anthropology: Theory, Politics, Praxis, and Poetics.* New Brunswick, NJ: Rutgers University Press, 2001.

McGuire, John Thomas. "'The Most Unjust Piece of Legislation': Section 213 of the Economy Act of 1932 and Feminism During the New Deal." *Journal of Policy History* 20, no. 4 (October 2008): 516–41. doi:10.1353/jph.0.0026.

Moraga, Cherríe, and Gloria Anzaldúa, eds. *This Bridge Called My Back: Writings by Radical Women of Color.* Watertown, MA: Persephone Press, 1981.

Morris, Aldon D. *The Origins of the Civil Rights Movement: Black Communities Organizing for Change.* New York: The Free Press, 1986.

Nash, Jennifer C. *Black Feminism Reimagined: After Intersectionality.* Durham, NC: Duke University Press, 2019.

National Woman's Party. *Black Women in America: Contributors to Our Heritage.* Washington, DC: Sewall-Belmont House and Museum, 2003.

Oluo, Ijeoma. *So You Want to Talk about Race.* New York: Seal Press, 2018.

Osselaer, Heidi J. *Winning Their Place: Arizona Women in Politics, 1883–1950.* Tucson: University of Arizona Press, 2011.

———. "Women's Suffrage and Arizona's Quest for Statehood." *Territorial Times* 5, no. 1 (Fall 2011): 24–30. www.prescottcorral.org/wpcontent/uploads/2018/12/TerritorialTimes_V9.pdf.

Parker, Alison M. *Unceasing Militant: The Life of Mary Church Terrell.* Chapel Hill: The University of North Carolina Press, 2020.

Pollak, Ruth. *One Woman, One Vote.* PBS, 1995.

Register, Cheri. "When Women Went Public: Feminist Reforms in the 1970s." *Minnesota History* 61, no. 2 (Summer 2008): 62–75.

Roberts, Rebecca Boggs. *Suffragists in Washington, D.C.: The 1913 Parade and the Fight for the Vote.* American Heritage. Charleston, SC: History Press, 2017.

Rupp, Leila J., and Verta A. Taylor. *Survival in the Doldrums: The American Women's Rights Movement, 1945 to the 1960s.* Columbus: Ohio State University Press, 1990.

Salvatore, Susan Cianci, ed. *Civil Rights in America: Racial Voting Rights, a National Historic Landmarks Theme Study,* rev. ed. Washington, DC: National Park Service, 2009. www.nps.gov/subjects/tellingallamericansstories/upload/CivilRights_VotingRights.pdf.

Schuyler, Lorraine Gates. *The Weight of Their Votes: Southern Women and Political Leverage in the 1920s*. Chapel Hill: University of North Carolina Press, 2006.

Sherr, Lynn. *Failure Is Impossible: Susan B. Anthony in Her Own Words*. New York: Times Books, 1995.

Simon, Nina. *The Art of Relevance*. Santa Cruz, CA: Museum 2.0, 2016.

Solomon, Barbara Miller. *In the Company of Educated Women: A History of Women and Higher Education in America*. New Haven, CT: Yale University Press, 1985.

Spruill, Marjorie Julian. *Divided We Stand: The Battle Over Women's Rights and Family Values That Polarized American Politics*. New York: Bloomsbury, 2017.

———. *New Women of the New South: The Leaders of the Woman Suffrage Movement in the Southern States*. New York: Oxford University Press, 1993.

———, ed. *One Woman, One Vote: Rediscovering the Woman Suffrage Movement*. Troutdale, OR: NewSage Press, 1995.

Stevens, Doris. *Jailed for Freedom: American Women Win the Vote*. Edited by Carol O'Hare. Rev. ed. Troutdale, OR: NewSage Press, 1995.

Stuhler, Barbara. *For the Public Record: A Documentary History of the League of Women Voters*. Westport, CT: Greenwood Publishing Group, 2000.

Swinth, Kirsten. *Feminism's Forgotten Fight: The Unfinished Struggle for Work and Family*. Cambridge, MA: Harvard University Press, 2018.

Terborg-Penn, Rosalyn. *African American Women in the Struggle for the Vote, 1850–1920*. Bloomington: Indiana University Press, 1998.

Tetrault, Lisa. *The Myth of Seneca Falls: Memory and the Women's Suffrage Movement, 1848–1898*. Gender and American Culture. Chapel Hill: University of North Carolina Press, 2014.

Wadsworth, Sarah, and Wayne A. Wiegand. *Right Here I See My Own Books: The Woman's Building Library at the World's Columbian Exposition*. Studies in Print Culture and the History of the Book. Amherst: University of Massachusetts Press, 2012.

Wagner, Sally Roesch. *Sisters in Spirit: The Iroquois Influence on Early American Feminists*. Summertown, TN: Native Voices, 2001.

———. *A Time of Protest: Suffragists Challenge the Republic, 1870–1887*. Rev. ed. Yankton, SD: Sky Carrier Press, 1998.

———. *The Women's Suffrage Movement*. London: Penguin, 2019.

Ware, Susan. *Why They Marched: Untold Stories of the Women Who Fought for the Right to Vote*. Cambridge, MA: Harvard University Press, 2019.

Weber, Sandra. *The Woman Suffrage Statue: A History of Adelaide Johnson's Portrait Monument to Lucretia Mott, Elizabeth Cady Stanton and Susan B. Anthony at the United States Capitol*. Jefferson, NC: McFarland, 2016.

Weiss, Elaine F. *The Woman's Hour: The Great Fight to Win the Vote*. New York: Viking, 2018.

Welch, Phebe M., ed. *The General Federation of Women's Clubs: Eleventh Biennial Convention: Official Report*. Newark: The Federation, 1912.

Wellman, Judith. *The Road to Seneca Falls: Elizabeth Cady Stanton and the First Woman's Rights Convention*. Women, Gender, and Sexuality in American History. Urbana: University of Illinois Press, 2004.

Wells, Ida B. "Southern Horrors: Lynch Law in All Its Phases." In *Selected Works of Ida B. Wells-Barnett*, edited by Trudier Harris, 14–45. New York: Oxford University Press, 1991.

Zahniser, Jill Diane, and Amelia R. Fry. *Alice Paul: Claiming Power*. New York: Oxford University Press, 2014.

Index

Butler Center for Arkansas Studies of the Central Arkansas Library System (CALS), 8, 10

Cable Act, 105
California, 15, 23, 104. *See also* San Francisco, CA
Catt, Carrie Chapman, 12, 39, 44, 105
Chicago, IL, 23, 40, 44, 52, 104. *See also* Wells, Ida B.
Chick History: community dialogue and, 84; digitization and, 78–80; founding of, 77; funding and, 74; "March to the Nineteenth," 3, 78; methodology and, 80–81; research and, 73–75, 81–82, 97. *See also* Price, Rebecca
Chinese Exclusion Act (1882), 103, 106
churches, 18, 74, 79
Ciani, Kyle, 55
citizenship: barriers to, 5, 18–20, 40; expanding the narrative and, 3, 11–12, 14, 27–28, 73. *See also* Chinese Exclusion Act; Fifteenth Amendment; Fourteenth Amendment; Indian Citizenship Act; National Association of Colored Women; Nineteenth Amendment; Seneca Falls Women's Rights Convention; Voting Rights Act of 1965
citizenship schools, 18, 21
Civil Rights Act (1964), 21, 106
class: General Federation of Women's Clubs and, 34, 39–40, 43, 45–46; inclusive narratives and, 79, 91; reproductive rights and, 103; rise of the middle class, 21; suffrage movement and, 8, 27, 34, 61–62, 104. *See also* intersectionality
Combahee River Collective, 24, 107
Comisión Femenil Mexicana Nacional, 25
Congressional Union, 5, 50, 104–105
Constad, Alyssa, 34
critical race theory (CRT), 80–81

Democratic Party, 20, 106, 107
DiAngelo, Robin, 36, 98

Douglass, Frederick, 7, 56, 61, 102
DuBois, Ellen Carol, 27, 55

educational settings: Black women and, 18, 21, 43, 104; outreach to, 11–12, 14, 53. *See also* citizenship schools; sororities
educational programming: audiences for, 11–12, 14, 53; community dialogue and, 84–91; funding and, 10–11, 55–56, 68; inclusive narratives and, 4, 8–9, 53–54, 71–73, 77, 83–84, 91; incorporating new research, 3, 13; online, 34, 65, 111, 113; seventy-fifth anniversary and, 25; suffrage centennial and, 3, 10–11, 57–58, 67, 95–97. *See also* Chick History; Frances Willard House Museum; Frances Willard and Ida B. Wells Truth-Telling Project; General Federation of Women's Clubs; Nineteenth Amendment; research; Sewall-Belmont House and Museum
Equal Rights Amendment (ERA), 58n6, 105, 107; centennial of, 11; National Woman's Party and, 1, 2, 18, 34–35, 49, 52, 56, 58; opposition to, 23; President Jimmy Carter and, 25
ethnicity, 5, 24. *See also* immigration; men, Asian American; men, Hispanic and Latino; women, Asian American; women, Hispanic and Latino
Evanston, IL, 65–67. *See also* Frances Willard House Museum
exhibits: "100 Years after the 19th Amendment: Their Legacy, and Our Future," 10–11; centennial and, 3, 95–97; "Imagery and Irony," 9–10; inclusive narratives and, 4, 7–8, 11, 71–72, 83–84; online, 34, 65; "Rightfully Hers," 11; "Shall Not Be Denied," 96; seventy-fifth anniversary and, 25; "Standing Together," 57–58; "Visions of Equality," 26; "Women Win the Vote," 24. *See also* Chick History; educational programming; Frances Willard and Ida B. Wells Truth-Telling Project; Nineteenth Amendment; research; Sewall-Belmont House and Museum

About the Author

Page Harrington is a public historian specializing in early twentieth-century women's history. Currently as the vice president of cultural assets for Girl Scouts of the USA, Harrington maintains their historic collection and advises the Juliette Gordon Low Birthplace in Savannah, Georgia. As president of Page Harrington & Company, LLC, she helps museums integrate women's history into their existing museum content. She is the former executive director of the National Woman's Party at the Belmont-Paul Women's Equality National Monument. She serves on the Women's History Affinity Community for AASLH, the Women's Vote Centennial Initiative, and she was on the scholar committee for the U.S. Congressional Commission's exploratory study for an American Museum of Women's History. Harrington holds two master's degrees from the University of San Diego—one in public history and historic preservation and the second in nonprofit management and leadership.

About the Contributors

Alyssa Constad spent four years in Washington, DC, as the Women's History and Resource Center (WHRC) manager for the General Federation of Women's Clubs (GFWC). As the WHRC manager, Alyssa acted as GFWC's chief historian, archivist, and research librarian, and worked to make their collections a ubiquitous part of U.S. women's history. In 2017 Alyssa was awarded the National Council on Public History's New Professional Award for her work at GFWC. Alyssa earned her MA in public history from the University of South Carolina, where she focused on the history of the American Civil Rights Movement and twentieth-century protest movements. She earned her BA in American studies from Dickinson College. Alyssa currently works at Carpenters' Hall for the Carpenters' Company of the City and County of Philadelphia.

Jennifer Krafchik is currently the collections manager in the Office of Senate Curator. She is the former director of collections and deputy director of the National Woman's Party at the Belmont-Paul Women's Equality National Monument. Throughout her career, Krafchik has been responsible for directing administrative and day-to-day operations, exhibitions and interpretation, collections care, and public programs. Her work regularly includes projects that seek to provide widespread physical and online access to historic and educational resources. Krafchik has a master's of library and information science from the Catholic University of America and a bachelor of arts in history, specializing in American women's history, from Marymount University.

Lori Osborne is director of the Frances Willard House Museum and executive director of the Center for Women's History and Leadership, which manages the Willard House and the Woman's Christian Temperance Union Archives. She also directs the Evanston Women's History Project at the Evanston History Center. Osborne serves on the board of the National Collaborative for Women's History Sites (NCWHS) and in 2020 was the Illinois coordinator for the Votes for Women Trail, which was a NCWHS project in honor of the 100th anniversary of the Nineteenth (Suffrage) Amendment. Osborne holds a master's degree in English literature from the University of Chicago and a master's degree in public history from Loyola University Chicago.

Rebecca Price is a public historian with two decades of experience specializing in women's history. She holds an MA in museums studies from George Washington University and has worked for the National Museum of Women in the Arts, the Institute of Museums and Library Services, and the American Association for State and Local History (AASLH). In 2015, Price founded Chick History, a nonprofit organization dedicated to rebuilding history one story at a time by focusing on women's history, original programming, and community outreach. Chick History is committed to preserving and interpreting all women's histories and experiences through its unique programs and community-driven projects.